Contents

Introduction

The intention of the *QFINANCE Calculation Toolkit* is to bring together in one place all of the tools you need to be successful in business and professional finance today, from the accounts payable turnover ratio to the z-score, and present them in a simple and accessible way.

Each of the articles carefully explains what is being measured, its importance and practical application, and tricks of the trade, which provides the reader with pointers on interpreting the results. They also provide where appropriate cross-references to other articles in the book, plus links to further reading on the topic in question, both in print and on the web.

Written by specialists, they provide essential mathematical calculations for target setting and maintaining standards within an enterprise. They address not only key management questions on the day-to-day financial welfare of a business, but also provide indicators that can impact on strategic decision making. They will help you apply the theory to real-world business situations.

But reader beware, numbers are only a reflection of a firm's financial health at any given moment in time, so it is essential to understand the dynamics that sit behind the figures—and the direction they are moving in.

Accounts Payable Turnover Ratio

WHAT IT MEASURES

The rate at which a company pays off its suppliers. The accounts payable turnover ratio is a short-term liquidity measure that quantifies how well a company pays its average payable amount over a single accounting period.

WHY IT IS IMPORTANT

Investors want to know how quickly your company pays its bills, which is why the accounts payable turnover ratio is important. This ratio measures your company's short-term liquidity. Investors consider a falling ratio a sign that the company is taking longer to pay suppliers than before, which might suggest cash flow problems. However, a rising ratio would suggest a relatively short time between purchase of goods and services and payment.

HOW IT WORKS IN PRACTICE

The accounts payable turnover ratio is based on the total purchases made from suppliers, divided by the average accounts payable amount over the same period, as below:

$$\text{APTR} = \frac{\text{Total supplier purchases}}{\text{Average accounts payable}}$$

For example, if a company makes $10 million in purchases from suppliers during a year, and at any given point is owed an average $2 million in accounts payable, then the accounts payable turnover ratio for the period would be 5.

TRICKS OF THE TRADE

- Most companies are required to settle accounts within 30 days to avoid damaging credit relationships, meaning there are 12 risk-free cycles in any year. A ratio of 6 suggests a company is paying its bills less often than is possible, while a ratio above 12 suggests the opposite.

- On its own, the ratio does not tell investors a great deal. The accounts payable turnover ratio must be compared against the industry average to see if the business is competitive. In addition, the ratio should be tracked over successive accounting periods to provide insight into cash flow.
- A falling accounts payable turnover ratio may suggest one of two scenarios. First, the business might be experiencing cash flow problems or disputed invoices with suppliers, which leads to slower payment. However, a successful business may extend payments to make the best possible use of cash and might have negotiated more favorable payment terms with suppliers. Additional analysis is therefore advised when faced with a changing accounts payable turnover ratio.
- An alternative approach that some experts believe is more intuitive than accounts payable turnover ratio is "days payable outstanding." This expresses turnover as the average length of time in days between purchase of goods and services, and payment. To calculate days payable outstanding, simply divide the accounts payable turnover ratio by 365.

MORE INFO

Book:

White, Gerald I., Ashwinpaul C. Sondhi, and Dov Fried. *The Analysis and Use of Financial Statements*. 3rd ed. Chichester, UK: Wiley, 2003.

Article:

Cars, Andreas. "Dynamic current ratio: What it is and how to use it." *Investopedia*. Online at: www.investopedia.com/articles/02/090302.asp

Accounts Receivable Turnover

One of several measures used to assess operating performance, accounts receivable turnover also helps in appraising a company's credit policy and its cash flow.

WHAT IT MEASURES

The number of times in each accounting period, typically a year, that a company converts credit sales into cash.

WHY IT IS IMPORTANT

A high turnover figure is desirable because it indicates that a company collects revenues effectively, and that its customers pay bills promptly. A high figure also suggests that a company's credit and collection policies are sound.

In addition, the measurement is a reasonably good indicator of cash flow, and of overall operating efficiency.

HOW IT WORKS IN PRACTICE

The formula for accounts receivable turnover is straightforward. Simply divide the average amount of receivables into annual credit sales:

$$\text{Receivables turnover} = \frac{\text{Sales}}{\text{Receivables}}$$

If, for example, a company's sales are $4.5 million and its average receivables are $375,000, its receivables turnover is:

$$\frac{4{,}500{,}000}{375{,}000} = 12$$

TRICKS OF THE TRADE

- It is important to use the average amount of receivables over the period considered. Otherwise, receivables could be misleading for a company whose products are seasonal or are sold at irregular intervals.

- The measurement is also helpful to a company that is designing or revising credit terms.
- Accounts receivable turnover is among the measures that comprise asset utilization ratios, also called activity ratios.

MORE INFO

Book:

Salek, John G. *Accounts Receivable Management: Best Practices*. Hoboken, NJ: Wiley, 2005.

See Also:

Asset Utilization (pp. 29–31)

Accrual Rate

WHAT IT MEASURES

In the pensions world, accrual rate is the rate at which an individual's entitlement to pension benefit builds up related to his or her salary, often in an employer's pension scheme.

WHY IT IS IMPORTANT

It enables an individual to receive a pension benefit that is predictable and fair, while also providing employers with a simple way to predict the potential liabilities of a pension scheme. If your organization's pension is based on an accrual rate, employees earn (or "accrue") a monthly pension amount each year they work. If the employee earns a full pension, they will receive the sum of all those annual accruals as the total pension amount. The higher the accrual, the higher the eventual pension pay-out.

HOW IT WORKS IN PRACTICE

Accrual rates are usually expressed as a fraction of final pay. They vary between different countries and industry sectors, but are generally between 1/50 and 1/80. In the case of an accrual rate of 1/60, this means the employee receives 1/60th of their pensionable earnings for each year of eligible service. To calculate the pension of an employee who retires at the age of 58 after 30 years service on a final salary of $70,000, apply this formula including the accrual rate:

$$\text{Pension liability} = \text{Accrual rate} \times \text{Final salary} \times \text{Years of service}$$

So, in this case the pension liability is:

$$\frac{1}{60} \times \$70,000 \times 30 = \$35,000$$

The lower the denominator in an accrual rate, the higher the accrued benefits for each year of eligible service. So an accrual rate of 1/50 would create a different result:

$$\frac{1}{50} \times \$70,000 \times 30 = \$42,000$$

TRICKS OF THE TRADE

- Accrual rate can be applied to an employee's "final" salary, or may sometimes be applied to what is known as the "best five"—the average of the five highest salaries an employee earns over their entire eligible years of service.
- An accelerated accrual is one that is higher than the typical 1/60 and 1/80 found in occupational pension schemes. They are most frequently used in the public sector.
- An accrual rate can sometimes be expressed as a percentage, such as 1.25% (which is equivalent to 1/80).
- Accrual rates can also be expressed as dollar amounts rather than percentages or fractions. These schemes tend to be less advantageous for employees, since the employer's contribution is not tied to the employee's salary and will not necessarily increase at the same pace.
- Accrual rates can be applied to other employee benefits (commonly holiday and sick pay), but may also be used to refer to the interest added to certain sorts of mortgage loans.

Acid-Test Ratio

A second liquidity ratio that evaluates creditworthiness, the acid-test ratio stands as a more stringent test than the current ratio, hence its name.

WHAT IT MEASURES

How quickly a company's assets can be turned into cash, which is why assessment of a company's liquidity is also known as the quick ratio, or simply the acid ratio.

WHY IT IS IMPORTANT

Regardless of how this ratio is labeled, it is considered a highly reliable indicator of a company's financial strength and its ability to meet its short-term obligations. Because inventory can sometimes be difficult to liquidate, the acid-test ratio deducts inventory from current assets before they are compared with current liabilities—which is what distinguishes it from the current ratio.

Potential creditors like to use the acid-test ratio because it reveals how a company would fare if it had to pay off its bills under the worst possible conditions. Indeed, the assumption behind the acid-test ratio is that creditors are howling at the door demanding immediate payment, and that an enterprise has no time to sell off its inventory, or any of its stock.

HOW IT WORKS IN PRACTICE

The acid-test ratio's formula can be expressed in two ways, but both essentially reach the same conclusion. The more common expression is:

$$\text{Acid-test ratio} = \frac{(\text{Current assets} - \text{Inventory})}{\text{Current liabilities}}$$

If, for example, current assets total $7,700, inventory amounts to $1,200, and current liabilities total $4,500, then:

$$\frac{(7{,}700 - 1{,}200)}{4{,}500} = 1.44$$

A variation of this formula ignores inventory altogether, distinguishes assets as cash, receivables, and short-term investments, and then divides the sum of the three by the total current liabilities:

$$\text{Acid-test ratio} = \frac{(\text{Cash} + \text{Accounts receivable} + \text{Short-term investments})}{\text{Current liabilities}}$$

If, for example, cash totals $2,000, receivables total $3,000, short-term investments total $1,000, and liabilities total $4,800, then:

$$\frac{(2{,}000 + 3{,}000 + 1{,}000)}{4{,}800} = 1.25$$

There are two other ways to appraise liquidity, although neither is as commonly used: the cash ratio is the sum of cash and marketable securities divided by current liabilities; net quick assets is determined by adding cash, accounts receivable, and marketable securities, then subtracting current liabilities from that sum.

TRICKS OF THE TRADE

- In general, the quick ratio should be 1:1 or better. This means that a company has at least a unit's worth of easily convertible assets for each unit of its current liabilities. A high quick ratio usually reflects a sound, well-managed organization in no danger of imminent collapse, even in the extreme and unlikely event that its sales ceased immediately. On the other hand, companies with ratios of less than 1 could not pay their current liabilities, and should be looked at with extreme care.
- While a ratio of 1:1 is generally acceptable to most creditors, acceptable quick ratios vary by industry, as do almost all financial ratios. No ratio, in fact, is especially meaningful without knowledge of the business from which it originates. For example, a declining quick ratio with a stable current ratio may indicate that a company has built up too much inventory; but it could also suggest that the company has greatly improved its collection system.

- Some experts regard the acid-test ratio as an extreme version of the working capital ratio because it uses only cash and equivalents, and excludes inventory. An acid-test ratio that is notably lower than the working capital ratio often means that inventory makes up a large proportion of current assets. An example would be retail stores.
- Comparing quick ratios over an extended period of time can be used to signal developing trends in a company. While modest declines in the quick ratio do not automatically spell trouble, uncovering the reasons for changes can help to find ways to nip potential problems in the bud.
- Like the current ratio, the quick ratio is a snapshot, and a company can manipulate its figures to make it look robust at a given point in time.
- Investors who suddenly become keenly interested in a company's quick ratio may signal their anticipation of a downturn in the company's business or in the general economy.

MORE INFO

See Also:

Current Ratio (pp. 93–94)
Liquidity Ratio Analysis (pp. 163–165)

Activity-Based Costing

GETTING STARTED

Activity-based costing (ABC) attempts to create the big picture—crystal-clear, full, and accurate—by painting assorted little pictures.

- ABC identifies the relationship between a business activity and all the resources needed to conduct it by assigning costs to each of those resources, thus presenting the true total expense of the entire activity.
- ABC can account for so-called "soft," or indirect, operating costs, and thus produce a more revealing, and perhaps startlingly different, financial picture than other accounting methodologies such as standard costing might offer.
- Used properly, ABC helps management to distinguish operations that add value from those that do not, permitting more informed decisions about such matters as pricing, product mix, capital investments, and organizational change.
- In turn, ABC's advocates praise it as a more effective tool to identify and control costs, improve productivity, and increase profits.

FAQS

When did ABC start?

ABC came of age in the 1980s amid manufacturers' furious efforts to raise the quality of their products while simultaneously eliminating every unnecessary cost from their operations. The dramatic improvements realized by manufacturers have led to ABC becoming a widely used tool, especially in the manufacturing industry.

What are the basic steps of ABC?

There are five:

1. identify the product or service to be studied;
2. determine all the resources and processes that are required to create the product or deliver the service, and their respective costs;
3. determine the "cost drivers" for each resource: the cost of labor as well as raw materials;

4 collect costs and other data, such as time taken, for each process and resource;
5 use the data to calculate the overall cost of the product or service.

What are ABC's principal advantages?
First, ABC can gauge virtually any activity, be it a manufacturing process, a business process, the performance of a service, or an administrative operation. Second, it considers a much wider variety of resources and materials than more traditional accounting methodologies, and can thus present a more complete picture.

What are ABC's primary weaknesses?
It can be a very time-consuming exercise because of the volume of data it demands. Also, if not managed properly, ABC can transform every manager into an accountant whose energies become fixed on tracking the costs of the activity, rather than on tracking and perfecting the activity itself.

What kind of business sectors use ABC?
The list ranges from accountants to zoologists. It may be especially helpful for knowledge-based businesses that rely primarily on human services and related resources, whose total costs may be difficult to measure with more traditional accounting yardsticks.

What is critical to ABC's success?
Without gaining and maintaining the enduring commitment of all individuals, even a modestly detailed initiative will probably fail. It's also best to start with pilot projects to demonstrate success.

What preliminary steps are needed?
First, an organization must understand its activities and the resources that these require. Second, it must understand thoroughly the amount of information required, and the expense of generating that information. It must also determine what level of accuracy will be acceptable.

MAKING IT HAPPEN

Creating an ABC cost accounting system requires three preliminary steps:

1 converting to an accrual basis of accounting;
2 defining cost centers and cost allocation;
3 determining process and procedure costs.

Businesses have traditionally relied on the cash basis of accounting, which recognizes income when received and expenses when paid. ABC's foundation is the accrual basis. The numbers this statement presents are assigned to the various procedures performed during a given period. Cost centers are a company's identifiable products and services, but also include specific and detailed tasks within these broader activities. Defining cost centers will of course vary by business and method of operation. What is critical to ABC is the inclusion of all activities and all resources. Once these steps have been taken, the results are often more than satisfying.

Banks and financial services firms, for example, have long used ABC-like methods to confirm that investments in automated teller machines would be both cheaper than continuing to rely on tellers and clerks and would be in their customers' best interests.

Railroad companies have used the methodology to determine the cost of processing bills of lading by hand, fax, and the internet. Studying such costs confirmed the wisdom of using e-commerce, generating annual savings of up to $1 million.

Publishers launching "new media" services can more accurately calculate the true costs of creating material for them, then compare such costs to those required to produce traditional publications, and draw more accurate conclusions about what best serves their long- and short-term interests.

Law firms are better positioned to confirm that the hourly fees they charge—no matter how princely they may at first appear—do, in fact, enable them to provide their services profitably.

Finally, healthcare providers use ABC to measure profitability, eliminate unnecessary costs, and plan for change. A medical practice that knows the actual cost of providing a specific service, for example, can make far better decisions about the price of managed health care.

For instance, let's say the Apple-a-Day Medical Clinic includes three physicians, Drs Peel, Core, and Stem. Their clinic has an in-house laboratory and a radiology department. All direct revenues and expenses are allocated to the physician who performs the service and incurs the expense. Indirect variable overhead costs are allocated to each physician based on the proportion of total revenues that each generates in a given period. Fixed overhead costs are divided equally among physicians. Because of their respective incomes and expense allocations, each physician would represent a separate cost center.

Additional cost centers for this medical practice could be laboratory, radiology, and administration. As cost centers are defined, they could further be classified as, say, "patient service centers" or "support centers." In this example, laboratory, radiology, and each individual physician's activity would be patient service centers, while administration would be a support center.

Once cost centers are identified, management teams can begin studying the activities each one engages in and allocating the expenses each one incurs, including the cost of employee services. In this healthcare scenario, activities would range from actual treatment by physicians and nurses, X-rays, medical tests and assessments of their results, plus such administrative support services as personnel, bookkeeping, rent, utilities, property insurance, office supplies, advertising, telecommunications expenses, and equipment costs related to the administrative function. Rent, utilities, and property insurance are usually allocated on the basis of the square footage that the particular activity covers.

Tracking and allocating the detailed costs of individual activities and procedures can be accomplished by different methods, with various degrees of accuracy. The more detailed the cost analysis, of course, the greater the accuracy of the data. Then again, as the detail increases, so does the time and expense.

The most appropriate method is developed from time studies and direct expense allocation. Management teams that choose this method will need to devote several months to data collection in order to generate sufficient information to establish the personnel components of each activity's total cost. The cost of this exercise itself can be significant, but also worthwhile. Proponents say ABC has resulted in cost savings worth as much as 14 times the cost of the exercise. More importantly, the exercise has provided solid documentation for decisions that "seemed correct," as a Chrysler Corporation team once reported, "but could not be supported with hard evidence."

Time studies establish the average amount of time required to complete each task, plus best- and worst-case performances. Only those resources actually used are factored into the cost computation; unused resources are reported separately. These studies can also advise management how best to monitor and allocate expenses which might otherwise be expressed as part of general overhead, or go undetected altogether.

Notably, determining how much of an operation's personnel is underused or unused can significantly help management planning, specifically by exposing activities that are overstaffed or understaffed. This can be especially helpful to any knowledge-based business, since payroll is almost always its highest cost. Moreover, in any business, the more efficiently an enterprise deploys its personnel, the more profitable it will be.

In addition, this type of analysis can also establish useful performance benchmarks within an operation, and might even allow for a comparison of procedure costs with industry averages.

COMMON MISTAKES

Getting Caught Up in the Details

Notwithstanding its successes, ABC remains a tool, not an end in itself. Organizations can lose sight of that fact if they are not careful, and end up allowing it to dominate their working lives.

The enormity and complexity of such a project should never be underestimated. The data requirements alone are daunting. It is all too easy to get caught up in ABC's details and mechanics. In turn, estimating some costs is often recommended, to minimize the level of detail.

At the same time, however, some details are important prerequisites of objectivity and success. For example, if time studies are not used, some other measure must be used to allocate personnel and related costs, as well as indirect costs such as percentage of revenues or income, or the number of customer calls. These methods require far less time for compiling data and are less costly, but drawbacks abound. For one thing, accuracy suffers, and they are almost always subjective, potentially to the point of compromising the entire initiative. Being far less precise, these alternative methods do not differentiate between used and unused personnel resources, and will not provide information on unused capacity or trends in procedure costs.

Without the aid of computer software that has been developed to automate the process, ABC can be hopelessly time-consuming. Indeed, unaided by technology, ABC might well be hoist with its own petard and exposed as an outrageous waste of time.

Like any cost accounting system, activity-based costing is not static. Once established, it needs to be maintained and updated as business conditions and organizations change.

Finally, in delivering its crystal-clear pictures, activity-based costing also has the potential to make individual champions of particular products or services squirm, because it may reveal them to be far more expensive than they might otherwise appear. All the more reason for advocating caution: "Watch out what you wish for!" If a management team is to reduce and eliminate costs, it must first identify them and grasp their impact on specific processes or products. Because activity-based costing can paint a single picture that reveals all the individual direct and indirect costs a business incurs in a given operation, it can be a powerful tool for both assessing current operations and guiding prompt and intelligent reactions as circumstances change. In fact, it's also known as activity-based management (ABM).

MORE INFO

Books:

Burk, Karen B., and Douglas W. Webster. *Activity Based Costing and Performance*. Fairfax, VA: American Management Systems, 1994.

Grossman, Theodore, and John Leslie Livingstone. *The Portable MBA in Finance and Accounting*. 4th ed. Hoboken, NJ: Wiley, 2009.

Article:

Ness, Joseph A., and Thomas G. Cucuzza. "Tapping the full potential of ABC." *Harvard Business Review* (July/August 1995). Online at: tinyurl.com/np4zzv9

Website:

Activity Based Costing Association (ABCA™): abcbenchmarking.com

Alpha and Beta Values of a Security

Both alpha and beta are investment measures used to quantify risk and reward.

WHAT THEY MEASURE

A security's performance, adjusted for risk, compared to overall market behavior.

WHY THEY ARE IMPORTANT

Just as coaches would expect their most accomplished athletes to perform at a higher level than others, investors expect more from higher-risk investments. Alpha and beta give investors a quick indication of just how risky a stock or fund is.

Alpha is defined as "the return a security or a portfolio would be expected to earn if the market's rate of return were zero."

Beta is a means of measuring the volatility (or risk) of a stock or fund in comparison with the market as a whole. The beta of a stock or fund can be any value, positive or negative, but usually is between +0.25 and +1.75.

Alpha expresses the difference between the return expected from a stock or mutual fund, given its beta rating, and the return actually produced. A stock or fund that returns more than its beta would predict has a positive alpha, while one that returns less than the amount predicted by beta has a negative alpha. A large positive alpha indicates a strong performance, while a large negative alpha indicates a dismal performance.

HOW THEY WORK IN PRACTICE

To begin with, the market itself is assigned a beta of 1.0. If a stock or fund has a beta of 1.2, this means its price is likely to rise or fall by 12% when the overall market rises or falls by 10%; a beta of 0.7 means the stock or fund price is likely to move up or down at 70% of the level of the market change.

In practice, an alpha of 0.4% means the stock or fund in question outperformed the market-based return estimate by 0.4%. An alpha of −0.6% means the return was 0.6% less than would have been predicted from the change in the market alone.

Both alpha and beta should be readily available on request from investment firms, because the figures appear in standard performance reports. It is always best to ask for them, because calculating a stock's alpha rating requires first knowing a stock's beta rating, and calculating beta is a challenge! It is based on linear regression analysis, the week-to-week percentage changes in the given stock's price, and the corresponding week-to-week percentage price change in a market index, over a given period of time, often 24 to 36 months. In short, beta calculations can involve mathematical complexities.

If it's any consolation, calculating alpha is far less taxing, provided the requisite data are available. The formula is:

$$\text{Alpha} = \text{Actual return} - \text{Risk-free return} - \text{Beta} \times (\text{Index return} - \text{Risk-free return})$$

If a mutual fund with a beta rating of 1.1 returned 35%, while its benchmark index returned 30%, and a US Treasury bill returned 4% (T-bill returns are usually used as the "risk-free investment"), then the fund's alpha would equal 2.4%, based on the formula:

$$\begin{aligned} 35\% - 4\% - 1.1 \times (30\% - 4\%) &= 31\% - 1.1 \times 26\% \\ &= 31\% - 28.6\% \\ &= 2.4\% \end{aligned}$$

TRICKS OF THE TRADE

- The underlying rationale for both alpha and beta is that the return of a stock or mutual fund should at least exceed that of a "risk-free" investment such as a US Treasury bill.
- Stocks of many utilities have a beta of less than 1. Conversely, most high-tech, NASDAQ-based stocks have a beta greater than 1; they offer a higher rate of return but are also risky.
- Alpha is often used to assess the performance of a portfolio manager. However, a low alpha score doesn't necessarily reflect poor performance by a fund manager, any more than a high alpha score means that a manager's performance is outstanding. At times, factors beyond a manager's control affect alpha values.

MORE INFO

Reports:

Schwab Performance Technologies. "Troubleshooting an incorrect alpha." September 13, 2012. Online at: tinyurl.com/q4cza7j [PDF].

Schwab Performance Technologies. "Troubleshooting an incorrect beta." July 9, 2012. Online at: tinyurl.com/opb7qel [PDF].

Amortization

Amortization is often regarded as being the same as depreciation, but although the two accounting practices can be difficult to distinguish, there are differences between them. Amortization is also used in connection with loans, although that is not the primary focus here.

WHAT IT MEASURES

Amortization is a method of recovering (deducting or writing off) the capital costs of intangible assets over a fixed period of time. Its calculation is virtually identical to the straight-line method of depreciation.

Amortization also refers to the establishment of a schedule for repaying the principal and interest on a loan in equal amounts over a period of time. Because computers have made this a simple calculation, business references to amortization tend to focus more on the term's first definition.

WHY IT IS IMPORTANT

Amortization enables a company to identify its true costs, and thus its net income, more precisely. In the course of their business, most enterprises acquire intangible assets such as a patent for an invention, or a well-known brand or trademark. Since these assets can contribute to the revenue growth of the business, they can be—and are allowed to be—deducted against those future revenues over a period of years, provided the procedure conforms to accepted accounting practices.

For tax purposes, the distinction is not always made between amortization and depreciation, yet amortization remains a viable financial accounting concept in its own right.

HOW IT WORKS IN PRACTICE

Amortization is computed using the straight-line method of depreciation: divide the initial cost of the intangible asset by the estimated useful life of that asset. For example, if it costs $10,000 to acquire a patent and it has an estimated useful life of 10 years, the amortized amount per year is $1,000.

$$\frac{10{,}000}{10} = \$1{,}000 \text{ per year}$$

The amount of amortization accumulated since the asset was acquired appears on the organization's balance sheet as a deduction under the amortized asset.

While that formula is straightforward, amortization can also incorporate a variety of noncash charges to net earnings and/or asset values, such as depletion, write-offs, prepaid expenses, and deferred charges. Accordingly, there are many rules to regulate how these charges appear on financial statements. The rules are different in each country, and are occasionally changed, so it is necessary to stay abreast of them and rely on expert advice.

For financial reporting purposes, an intangible asset is amortized over a period of years. The amortizable life—"useful life"—of an intangible asset is the period over which it gives economic benefit. Several factors are considered when determining this useful life; for example, demand and competition, effects of obsolescence, legal or contractual limitations, renewal provisions, and service life expectations.

Intangibles that can be amortized include:

- **Copyrights**, based on the amount paid either to purchase them or to develop them internally, plus the costs incurred in producing the work (wages or materials, for example). At present, a copyright is granted for the life of the author plus 70 years. However, the estimated useful life of a copyright is usually far shorter than its legal life, and it is generally amortized over a fairly short period.
- **Cost of a franchise**, including any fees paid to the franchiser, as well as legal costs or expenses incurred in the acquisition. A franchise granted for a limited period should be amortized over its life. If the franchise has an indefinite life, it should be amortized over a reasonable period, not to exceed 40 years.

- **Covenants not to compete**: an agreement by the seller of a business not to engage in a competing business in a certain area for a specific period of time. The cost of the not-to-compete covenant should be amortized over the period covered by the covenant unless its estimated economic life is expected to be shorter.
- **Easement costs** that grant a right of way may be amortized if there is a limited and specified life.
- **Organization costs** incurred when forming a corporation or a partnership, including legal fees, accounting services, incorporation fees, and other related services. Organization costs are usually amortized over 60 months.
- **Patents**, both those developed internally and those purchased. If developed internally, a patent's "amortizable basis" includes legal fees incurred during the application process. Normally, a patent is amortized over its legal life, or over its remaining life if purchased. However, it should be amortized over its legal life or its economic life, whichever is the shorter.
- **Trademarks, brands, and trade names**, which should be written off over a period not to exceed 40 years. However, since the value of these assets depends on the changing tastes of consumers, they are frequently amortized over a shorter period.
- Other types of property that may be amortized include certain intangible drilling costs, circulation costs, mine development costs, pollution control facilities, and reforestation expenditures. They can even include intangibles such as the value of a market share or a market's composition: an example is the portion of an acquired business that is attributable to the existence of a given customer base.

TRICKS OF THE TRADE

- Certain intangibles cannot be amortized, but may be depreciated using a straight-line approach if they have a "determinable" useful life. Because the rules are different in each country and are subject to change, it is essential to rely on specialist advice.
- Computer software may be amortized under certain conditions, depending on its purpose. Software that is amortized is generally

given a 60-month life, but it may be amortized over a shorter period if it can clearly be established that it will be obsolete or no longer used within a shorter time.

- Under certain conditions, customer lists that were purchased may be amortized if it can be demonstrated that the list has a finite useful life, in that customers on the list are likely to be lost over a period of time.
- While leasehold improvements are depreciated for income tax purposes, they are amortized when it comes to financial reporting—either over the remaining term of the lease or their expected useful life, whichever is the shorter.
- Annual payments incurred under a franchise agreement should be expensed when incurred.
- The internet has many amortization loan calculators that can automatically determine monthly payment figures and the total cost of a loan.

MORE INFO

Websites:

Financial Accounting Standards Board (FASB): www.fasb.org

US Copyright Office: www.copyright.gov

US Patent and Trademark Office: www.uspto.gov

Annual Percentage Rate

Different investments typically offer different compounding periods, usually quarterly or monthly. The annual percentage rate, or APR, allows them to be compared over a common period of time, namely one year.

WHAT IT MEASURES

The APR measures either the rate of interest that invested money earns in one year, or the cost of credit expressed as a yearly rate.

WHY IT IS IMPORTANT

It enables an investor or borrower to compare like with like. When evaluating investment alternatives, naturally it's important to know which one will pay the greatest return. By the same token, borrowers want to know which loan alternative offers the best terms. Determining the annual percentage rate provides a direct comparison.

HOW IT WORKS IN PRACTICE

To calculate the APR, apply this formula:

$$\text{APR} = \left(1 + \frac{i}{m}\right)^m - 1$$

where *i* is the interest rate quoted, expressed as a decimal, and *m* is the number of compounding periods per year. For example, if a bank offers a 6% interest rate, paid quarterly, the APR would be calculated this way:

$$\begin{aligned}\left(1 + \frac{0.06}{4}\right)^4 - 1 &= (1 + 0.015)^4 - 1 \\ &= 1.015^4 - 1 \\ &= 1.0614 - 1 \\ &= 0.0614 \\ &= 6.14\%\end{aligned}$$

TRICKS OF THE TRADE

- As a rule of thumb, the annual percentage rate is slightly higher than the quoted rate.
- When using the formula, be sure to express the rate as a decimal (that is, 6% becomes 0.06).
- When expressed as the cost of credit, remember to include other costs of obtaining the credit in addition to interest, such as loan closing costs and financial fees.
- APR provides an excellent basis for comparing mortgage or other loan rates; lenders are required to disclose it.
- When used in the context of investment, APR can also be called the "annual percentage yield," or APY.

MORE INFO

See Also:

Fixed-Deposit Compound Interest (pp. 145–146)
Nominal and Real Interest Rates (pp. 182–184)

Asset Turnover

Another of the asset utilization ratios, asset turnover measures the productivity of assets. In some circles it is also referred to as the earning power of assets.

WHAT IT MEASURES

The amount of sales generated for every dollar's worth of assets over a given period.

WHY IT IS IMPORTANT

Asset turnover measures how well a company is leveraging its assets to produce revenue. A well-managed manufacturer, for example, will make its plant and equipment work hard for the business by minimizing idle time for machines.

The higher the number the better—within reason. As a rule of thumb, companies with low profit margins tend to have high asset turnover; those with high profit margins have low asset turnover.

This ratio can also show how capital intensive a business is. Some businesses, such as software developers, can generate tremendous sales per dollar of assets because their assets are modest. At the other end of the scale, electric utilities, heavy industry manufacturers, and even cable TV companies need a huge asset base to generate sales.

Finally, asset turnover serves as a tool to keep managers mindful of the company's balance sheet along with its profit and loss account.

HOW IT WORKS IN PRACTICE

Asset turnover's basic formula is simply sales divided by assets:

$$\frac{\text{Sales revenue}}{\text{Total assets}}$$

Most experts recommend using average total assets in the formula. To determine this figure, add total assets at the beginning of the year to total assets at the end of the year and divide by two.

If, for instance, annual sales totaled $4.5 million, and total assets were $1.84 million at the beginning of the year and $1.78 million at the year end, the average total assets would be $1.81 million, and the asset turnover ratio would be:

$$\frac{4{,}500{,}000}{1{,}810{,}000} = 2.49$$

A variation of the formula is:

$$\frac{\text{Sales revenue}}{\text{Fixed assets}}$$

If average fixed assets were $900,000, then asset turnover would be:

$$\frac{4{,}500{,}000}{900{,}000} = 5$$

TRICKS OF THE TRADE

- This ratio is especially useful for growth companies to gauge whether or not they are growing revenue (for example) turnover, in healthy proportion to assets.
- Asset turnover numbers are useful for comparing competitors within industries. Like most ratios, they vary from industry to industry. As with most numbers, the most meaningful comparisons are made over extended periods of time.
- Too high a ratio may suggest overtrading: too much sales revenue with too little investment. Conversely, too low a ratio may suggest undertrading and an inefficient management of resources.
- A declining ratio may be indicative of a company that overinvested in plant, equipment, or other fixed assets, or is not using existing assets effectively.

MORE INFO

See Also:

Asset Utilization (pp. 29–31)
Return on Assets (pp. 221–223)

Asset Utilization

Appraising asset utilization is a multi-task exercise conceived and performed in the spirit of "one manages what one measures." There is plenty to measure.

WHAT IT MEASURES

How efficiently an organization uses its resources and, in turn, the effectiveness of the organization's managers.

WHY IT IS IMPORTANT

The success of any enterprise is tied to its ability to manage and leverage its assets. Hefty sales and profits can hide any number of inefficiencies. By examining several relationships between sales and assets, asset utilization delivers a reasonably detailed picture of how well a company is being managed and led—certainly enough to call attention both to sources of trouble and to role-model operations.

Moreover, since all the figures used in this analysis are taken from a company's balance sheet or profit and loss statement, the ratios that result can be used to compare a company's performance with individual competitors and with industries as a whole.

Many companies use this measure not only to evaluate their aggregate success but also to determine compensation for managers.

HOW IT WORKS IN PRACTICE

Asset utilization relies on a family of asset utilization ratios, also called activity ratios. The individual ratios in the family can vary, depending on the practitioner. They include measures that also stand alone, such as accounts receivable turnover and asset turnover. The most commonly used sets of asset utilization ratios include these and the following measures.

Average collection period is also known as days sales outstanding. It links accounts receivable with daily sales and is expressed in number of days; the lower the number, the better the performance. Its formula is:

$$\text{Average collection period} = \frac{\text{Accounts receivable}}{\text{Average daily sales}}$$

For example, if accounts receivable are $280,000 and average daily sales are $7,000, then:

$$\frac{280{,}000}{7{,}000} = 40 \text{ days}$$

Inventory turnover compares the cost of goods sold (COGS) with inventory; for this measure, expressed in "turns," the higher the number the better. Its formula is:

$$\text{Inventory turnover} = \frac{\text{Cost of goods sold}}{\text{Inventory}}$$

For example, if COGS is $2 million and inventory at the end of the period is $500,000, then:

$$\frac{2{,}000{,}000}{500{,}000} = 4$$

Some asset utilization repertoires include ratios like debtor days, while others study the relationships listed below.

Depreciation/Assets measures the percentage of assets being depreciated to gauge how quickly product plants are aging and assets are being consumed.

Depreciation/Sales measures the percentage of sales that is tied up covering the wear and tear of the physical plant.

In either instance, a high percentage could be cause for concern.

Income/Assets measures how well management uses its assets to generate net income. It is the same formula as return on assets.

Income/Plant measures how effectively a company uses its investment in fixed assets to generate net income.

In these two instances, high numbers are desirable.

Plant/Assets expresses the percentage of total assets that is tied up in land, buildings, and equipment.

By themselves, of course, the individual numbers are meaningless. Their value lies in how they compare with the corresponding numbers of competitors and with industry averages. A company with an inventory turnover of 4 in an industry whose average is 7, for example, surely has room for improvement, because the comparison indicates that it is generating fewer sales per unit of inventory and is therefore less efficient than its competitors.

TRICKS OF THE TRADE

- Asset utilization is particularly useful to companies considering expansion or capital investment: if production can be increased by improving the efficiency of existing resources, there is no need to spend the sums expansion would cost.
- Like all families of ratios, no single number or comparison is necessarily cause for alarm or rejoicing. Asset utilization proves most beneficial over an extended period of time.
- Studying all measures at once can devour a lot of time, although computers have trimmed hours into seconds. Managements in smaller organizations may conduct asset utilization on a continuing basis, tracking particular measures monthly to stay abreast of operating trends.

MORE INFO

See Also:

Accounts Receivable Turnover (pp. 3–4)
Asset Turnover (pp. 26–28)
Days Sales Outstanding (pp. 95–97)

Basis Point Value

WHAT IT MEASURES

The basis point value (BPV) expresses the change in value of an asset or financial instrument that results from a 0.01 percentage change in yield. BPV is commonly used to measure interest rate risk, and may be referred to as a delta or DV01.

WHY IT IS IMPORTANT

Basis point value is extremely important in assessing the impact of changes to the value or rate of a financial instrument such as an asset or portfolio. Simply stating an absolute percentage can be unclear—a 1% increase to a 10% rate might refer to an increase to 10.1% or 11%, for example.

Basis points can be used to measure changes and differentials in interest rates and margins. For example, a floating interest rate might be set at 25 BPV above Libor. If Libor is 3.5%, this means the floating rate will be 3.75%. Basis points are also useful in describing margins, because percentage changes may be very small or unclear—even while they might have a considerable impact on the bottom line.

BPV is commonly used in financial markets to measure interest rates, and specifically the risk associated with a particular rate. It is popular because it is relatively simple to calculate and can be applied in any scenario where you have a known cash flow.

HOW IT WORKS IN PRACTICE

At its most basic, BPV is 1/100th of 1%. Therefore, there are 30 basis points between a bond with a yield of 10.3% and 10.6%. To calculate simple BPV, therefore, use this formula:

BPV = Yield × 0.0001, or 1% of 1%

It is often useful to take the calculation a step further to define the price value of a basis point (PVBP), which is the change in value of a bond or other financial instrument given a change of one basis point value. Sometimes this is also known as “dollar valuation of 01” or DV01.

To calculate PVBP, apply the following calculation:

PVBP = Initial price – Price if yield changes by 1 BPV

In the financial market, a basis point is used to refer to the yield that a bond or investment pays to the investor. For example, if a bond yield moves from 7.45% to 7.65%, it is said to have risen 20 basis points.

For example, if a bank raises interest rates from 2.5% to 2.75%, you would calculate PVBP as follows:

$0.25 \times 0.0001 \times 100 = 0.025\%$ change

(This is the difference in yield from the account created by a movement of 1 basis point).

TRICKS OF THE TRADE

- Large financial institutions use highly specialized and sophisticated computer systems to calculate the impact of basis point changes (the DV01 figure) in real-time. These figures can be calculated in spreadsheets, but they are difficult to produce accurately, particularly for complex bonds.
- In the bond market, a basis point is used to refer to the yield that a bond pays to the investor. For example, if a bond yield moves from 1.45% to 1.65%, it has risen 20 basis points. Investors will commonly compare bond yields by weighting them according to the BPV.

MORE INFO

Website:

Barbican Consulting guide to BPV: www.barbicanconsulting.co.uk/bpv

Binomial Distribution

WHAT IT MEASURES

This refers to the number of incidences of a specific outcome in a series of events or trials. For example, how many times you throw the number three when rolling a die 10 times.

WHY IT IS IMPORTANT

The binomial distribution is widely used to test statistical probabilities and significance, and is a good way of visually detecting unexpected values. It is a useful tool in determining permutations, combinations, and probabilities, where the outcomes can be broken down into two probabilities (p and q), where p and q are complementary (i.e., $p + q = 1$).

For example, tossing a coin has only two possible outcomes, heads or tails. Each of these outcomes has a theoretical probability of 0.5. Using the binomial expansion, showing all possible outcomes and combinations, the probability is represented as follows:

$(p+q)^2 = p^2 + 2pq + q^2$, or more simply, $pp + 2pq + qq$

If p is heads and q is tails, the theory shows there is only one way to get two heads (pp), two ways to get a head and a tail ($2pq$), and one way to get two tails (qq).

Common uses of binomial distributions in business include quality control, public opinion surveys, medical research, and insurance problems. It can be applied to complex processes such as sampling items in factory production lines or to estimate percentage failure rates of products and components.

HOW IT WORKS IN PRACTICE

If I toss a coin 100 times and there are 60 instances of heads and 40 of tails:

$n = 100$ (the number of opportunities where heads could occur)

$k = 60$ (the number of heads that did occur)

$p = 0.5$ (the statistical probability that heads would occur each time)

$q = 0.5$ (the complementary probability that tails would occur)

At this point, there are three ways to demonstrate probability using a binomial equation. In all three cases, k represents the number of times a specific outcome is observed, p is the probability of heads, and q is the complementary probability of tails.

Method 1

If $n = 100$, exact binomial probabilities can be calculated using repeated applications of the standard binomial formula, as below. This works out the probability of exactly k heads:

$$P(k) = \left[\frac{n!}{k!(n-k!)}\right] p^k q^{n-k}$$

This is considered to be the most accurate calculation of binomial probabilities, since it involves precise calculation. However, it is best used where n is less than 1,000, or where you are using a computer program to perform more complex calculations on larger sample sizes.

Method 2

If both np and nq are greater than 5, then binomial probabilities can be estimated using an approximation to the Normal distribution. This relies on the following formula:

$$Z = \frac{(k - m \pm 0.5)}{\text{sqrt}}$$

where:
$m = np$, or the mean of the binomial sampling distribution
sqrt = the standard deviation of the binomial sampling distribution

Method 3

The final method of estimating binomial distribution is the Poisson probability function, which is used where the number of occurrences (n) is less than 150, and the mean (np) and variance (npq) are within 10% of one another. In this case, you can repeatedly apply the Poisson formula to estimate binomial distribution, as below:

$$P(k \text{ out of } n) = \frac{(e - m)(mk)}{k!}$$

Do keep in mind that the results of the Poisson procedure are only approximations of the true binomial probabilities, valid only in the case that the binomial mean and variance are very close.

TRICKS OF THE TRADE

- To satisfy the requirements of binomial distribution, the event being studied must display certain characteristics:
  - the number of trials or occurrences are fixed
  - there are only two possible outcomes (heads/tails or win/lose, for example)
  - all occurrences are independent of each other (tossing a head does not make it more or less likely you will get the same result next time)
  - all outcomes have the same probability of success
- Binomial distribution is best applied in cases where the population size is at least 10 times the sample size, and not to simple random samples.
- To find probabilities from a binomial distribution, you can perform a manual calculation, but there are online calculators available, or you can use a binomial table or computer spreadsheet.
- The binomial distribution is sometimes called a Bernoulli experiment or trial.
- The binomial *probability* refers to the probability that a binomial experiment results in exactly *x* successes. In the example above, we see that the binomial probability of getting exactly one head in two coin flips is 0.5.
- A cumulative binomial probability refers to the probability that the binomial random variable falls within a specified range (for example, is greater than or equal to a stated lower limit and less than or equal to a stated upper limit).

MORE INFO

Websites:

Penn State University on binomial distribution (via Internet Archive): tinyurl.com/658qcex

Stat Trek binomial calculator: stattrek.com/online-calculator/binomial.aspx

Texas University binomial calculator: www.stat.tamu.edu/~west/applets/binomialdemo.html

Bond Yield

A bond is a certificate that promises to repay a sum of money borrowed, plus interest, on a specified date, usually years into the future. National, state, and local governments issue bonds, as do corporations and many institutions.

Short-term bonds generally mature in up to 3 years, intermediate-term bonds in 3 to 10 years, and long-term bonds in more than 10 years, with 30 years generally being the upper limit. Longer-term bonds are considered a higher risk because interest rates are certain to change during their lifetime, but they tend to pay higher interest rates to attract investors and reward them for the additional risk.

Bonds are traded on the open market, just like stocks. They are reliable economic indicators, but perform in the reverse direction to interest rates: if bond prices are rising, interest rates and stock markets are likely to be falling, while if interest rates have gone up since a bond was first issued, prices of new bonds will fall.

WHAT IT MEASURES

The annual return on this certificate (the rate of interest) expressed as a percentage of the current market price of the bond.

WHY IT IS IMPORTANT

Bonds can tie up investors' money for periods of up to 30 years, so knowing their yield is a critical investment consideration. Similarly, bond issuers need to know the price they will pay to incur their debt, so that they can compare it with the cost of other means of raising capital.

HOW IT WORKS IN PRACTICE

Bonds are issued in increments of $1,000. To calculate the yield amount, multiply the face value of the bond by the stated rate, expressed as a decimal. For example, buying a new 10-year $1,000 bond that pays 6% interest will produce an annual yield of $60:

$$1,000 \times 0.06 = \$60$$

The $60 will be paid as $30 every six months. At the end of 10 years, the purchaser will have earned $600, and will also be repaid the original $1,000. Because the bond was purchased when it was first issued, the 6% is also called the "yield to maturity."

This basic formula is complicated by other factors. First is the "time-value of money" theory: money paid in the future is worth less than money paid today. A more detailed computation of total bond yield requires the calculation of the present value of the interest earned each year. Second, changing interest rates have a marked impact on bond trading and, ultimately, on yield. Changes in interest rates cannot affect the interest paid by bonds already issued, but they do affect the prices of new bonds.

TRICKS OF THE TRADE

- **Yield to call**. Bond issuers reserve the right to "call," or redeem, the bond before the maturity date, at certain times and at a certain price. Issuers often do this if interest rates fall and they can issue new bonds at a lower rate. Bond buyers should obtain the yield-to-call rate, which may, in fact, be a more realistic indicator of the return expected.
- **Different types of bond**. Some bonds are backed by assets, while others are issued on the strength of the issue's good standing. Investors should know the difference.
- **Zero-coupon bonds**. These pay no interest at all, but are sold at a deep discount and increase in value until maturity. A buyer might pay $3,000 for a 25-year zero bond with a face value of $10,000. This bond will simply accrue value each year, and at maturity will be worth $10,000, thus earning $7,000. These are high-risk investments, however, especially if they must be sold on the open market amid rising interest rates.
- **Interest rates**. Bond values fall when interest rates rise, and rise when interest rates fall, because when interest rates rise existing bonds become less valuable and less attractive.

MORE INFO

See Also:

Current Price of a Bond (pp. 90–92)
Yield (pp. 275–276)

Book Value

No-nonsense number-crunchers adore this measure because it presents the value of common stock equity based on historical values and thus helps separate fact from fiction and fancy.

WHAT IT MEASURES

A company's common stock equity as it appears on a balance sheet.

WHY IT IS IMPORTANT

Book value represents a company's net worth to its stockholders, based on the difference between assets and liabilities plus debt. Typically, book value is substantially different from market value, especially in high-tech and knowledge-based industries whose primary assets are intangible and therefore do not appear on the balance sheet.

When compared with its market value, a company's book value helps to reveal how it is regarded by the investment community. A market value that is notably higher than book value indicates that investors have a high regard for the company. A market value that is, for example, a multiple of book value suggests that investors' regard may be unreasonably high—as was shown in the painful plunge of dot-com companies in 2000 and 2001.

The reverse is also true, of course; indeed, it may suggest that a company's stock is a bargain.

A companion measure is book value per stock. It shows the value of the company's assets that each stockholder theoretically would receive if a company were liquidated.

HOW IT WORKS IN PRACTICE

To calculate book value, subtract a company's liabilities and the value of its debt and preferred stock from its total assets. All of these figures appear on a company's balance sheet. For example:

Total assets	$1,300
Current liabilities	–$400
Long-term liabilities, preferred stock	–$250
Book value	**$650**

Book value per stock is calculated by dividing the book value by the number of stocks issued:

$$\text{Book value per stock} = \frac{\text{Book value}}{\text{Number of stocks issued}}$$

If our example is expressed in millions of dollars and the company has 35 million stocks outstanding, the book value per stock would be $650 million divided by 35 million:

$$\frac{650}{35} = \$18.57$$

TRICKS OF THE TRADE

- Related terms include:
  - adjusted book value or modified book value, which is book value after assets and liabilities are adjusted to market value
  - tangible book value, which also subtracts intangible assets, patents, trademarks, and the value of research and development
  - The rationale is that these items cannot be sold outright
- Book value can also mean the value of an individual asset as it appears on a balance sheet, in which case it is equal to the cost of the asset minus any accumulated depreciation.
- Though often considered a realistic appraisal, book value can still contain unrealistic figures. For example, a building might be fully depreciated and have no official asset value but could still be sold for millions, or four-year-old computer equipment that is not fully depreciated might have asset value but no market value, given its age and advances in technology.

MORE INFO

See Also:

Market/Book Ratio (pp. 174–175)

Borrowing Costs and Capitalization

Borrowing costs are the tangible costs of incurring debt, typically expressed in terms of annual interest paid on outstanding debt or as a stated, annual coupon rate. A firm's borrowing costs are a function of its credit quality. Credit quality is determined on the type of debt security issued, capital structure, and capital-intensity of the business. Understanding each of the components of credit quality provides a clear picture of the determinants of a company's cost of debt financing. Borrowing costs also include the expenses incurred to issue debt securities.

GETTING STARTED

The costs of borrowing are primarily made up of interest and issuance expenses. The interest rate assigned to a particular debt instrument is based on the level of default risk assumed by the investor. Several rating agencies assess the default risk of public debt issuances and provide a rating that is indicative of credit quality. The credit quality is greater for secured/collateralized senior debt than for unsecured subordinated debt issued by the same company, and hence the former typically carries a lower rate of interest. Companies that have higher levels of debt must typically pay higher interest rates to investors to compensate them for the increased risk of default. Capital-intensive businesses can usually maintain greater debt-to-capital ratios for the same level of borrowing costs than businesses that are less capital intensive.

FAQS

What are debt issuance costs and are they always incurred when borrowing money?

Debt issuance costs are the underwriting, legal, and administrative fees required to issue the debt. These fees are significant when issuing debt in the public markets, such as bonds. However, other types of debt, such as private placements or bank loans, are cheaper to issue because they require less underwriting, legal, and administrative support. Consequently, the public issuers of debt are typically *Fortune* 500 companies, while middle-market companies tend to issue debt through private placements.

Do borrowing costs increase or decrease for callable bonds or bonds with detachable stock warrants?

When debt securities are issued with a call feature, the debt can be retired at the discretion of the company until some specified future date. The call feature represents value to the issuing company, much like a call option on equity. The issuer must compensate investors for providing this option. Therefore, the interest rate on callable bonds is typically higher than those on noncallable bonds of the same credit quality. That is, the borrowing costs increase on bonds with a call feature.

The opposite is true of bonds with detachable stock warrants. A stock warrant provides the bondholder with the right to purchase shares of common stock in the issuing company at a specified price during a defined period of time. The warrant's strike price is typically at, or higher than, the current market price of the company's stock. Nonetheless, the warrant provides value to the bondholder in the form of a call option on the company's equity. Because these warrants add to the potential total return on the debt, the stated interest rate is usually lower than that on debt issued without warrants of similar credit quality. Borrowing costs are typically lower on bonds with detachable stock warrants.

MAKING IT HAPPEN

When companies borrow money, they enter a formal obligation to make periodic payments of interest and to repay the principal balance outstanding according to an agreed schedule. The interest payments are typically based on a stated, annual percentage of the original amount borrowed. The interest paid on such obligations represents the cost of borrowing, along with the costs to issue the debt.

The Difference between Funded and Unfunded Debt

The debt can be classified as funded or unfunded. Funded debt is long-term debt or debt that has a maturity date in excess of one year.

Unfunded debt is short-term debt requiring repayment within a year from issuance. Funded debt is usually issued in the public markets or in the form of a private placement to qualified institutional investors. Most unfunded debt is commercial paper or bank lines of credit.

Senior and Subordinated Debt

Debt can also be classified as senior or subordinated, based on its preference to assets in the event of default by the lender. Subordinated lenders have a junior claim to assets in the event of bankruptcy and are paid only after senior creditors' claims have been satisfied.

Senior credit can be secured or unsecured. Much of the corporate debt outstanding is referred to as a bond. However, a true bond is secured by claims against the company's property, plant, and equipment. For example, many airlines secure their public debt by mortgaging their airplanes. In this example, an airline could be forced to sell its airplanes to pay its public debt if it defaulted on the bonds. Most public debt is secured by the good faith and credit of the issuing company, and is more accurately called a debenture. A company can also pledge certain assets, like accounts receivable, inventory, or property, as collateral for a loan or debt.

Differing Levels of Risk

Even when debt is secured or collateralized, it still does not guarantee repayment by the issuer. A company's underlying asset value and its earnings may be very volatile, increasing the risk of default in a down business cycle. Because this risk can be different from one business to another, there are several national rating agencies that rate public debt based on the creditworthiness of the borrower. Investment-grade debt securities are securities that are rated in the top four categories of creditworthiness by Standard & Poor's or Moody's rating agencies. All debt securities rated below investment-grade are considered to be junk bonds.

Different Types of Interest Rate

Debt can have a fixed or floating rate of interest. Fixed-rate debt pays the same interest rate over its term. Most long-term debt is issued with a fixed rate. Many short-term loans are floating-rate instruments based on the prime lending rate, Libor (London Interbank Offered Rate), or some US Treasury security. When the rates on these securities change, the loan rate changes. For example, a line of credit whose current interest rate is 6%, based on one percentage point above the three-year Libor rate, will change to 6.25% if Libor increases by a quarter of a point. Floating-rate debt is typically used to support a business's working capital requirements.

The Determinants of Credit Quality

The interest rate and, consequently, the borrowing cost is determined by credit quality. Credit quality depends on the type of debt security, the amount of debt relative to total capital, and the capital-intensity of a company's business. All other things being equal, a secured or collateralized debt security is less risky than an unsecured obligation. Therefore, investors require a greater return for the additional risk assumed by investing in unsecured debt. Likewise, an investor will require a greater return for subordinated debt than for senior credit.

Credit quality also deteriorates as the level of debt grows on the balance sheet of a company. Intuitively, the greater the debt-to-capital ratio, the greater the risk of default. By continuing to add financial leverage to its business operations, a company increases the risks that in a bad year it may not be able to cover its debt service. In studies on cost of capital, it was determined that companies experiencing debt-to-capital ratios between 25% and 45% saw their cost of capital increase exponentially, indicating greater risk of financial distress.

Debt-to-Capital Ratios

Finally, companies that are more capital-intensive tend to have greater debt-to-capital ratios. For example, automobile and airline manufacturers typically maintain greater leverage than professional services and software companies. The academic explanation given for this circumstance is the degree of industry maturity, lower earnings volatility, and the ability to secure more debt with tangible assets. Consequently, companies in more capital-intensive industries tend to have lower borrowing costs at a given debt-to-capital ratio than those in less capital-intensive industries.

TRICKS OF THE TRADE

- The costs of borrowing are composed of interest payments and issuance costs. Interest paid on outstanding debt is a function of the creditworthiness of the borrower. The greater the interest rate on a debt security relative to other, similar securities, the lower the credit quality of the issuer. As credit quality falls below investment-grade, the risk of default becomes ominously greater and the costs of borrowing become more exorbitant.
- A company's capital structure is another major determinant of credit quality. There is a direct relationship between debt level and default risk. At a given debt to capital ratio, incremental borrowing costs increase dramatically as the company's risk of financial distress reaches its peak.

MORE INFO

Book:

Brealey, Richard A., Stewart C. Myers, and Franklin Allen. *Principles of Corporate Finance*. 11th ed. New York: McGraw-Hill, 2013.

See Also:

Debt/Capital Ratio (pp. 98–99)
Debt/Equity Ratio (pp. 100–102)

Break-Even Analysis

WHAT IT MEASURES

Break-even is the point at which a product or service stops costing money to produce and sell, and starts generating a profit for your business. This means sales have reached sufficient volume to cover the variable and fixed costs of producing and distributing your product.

WHY IT IS IMPORTANT

The ultimate goal of any business is to make money, but break-even analysis can also provide valuable information for profitable businesses in terms of setting price levels, targeting optimal variable/fixed price combinations and determining the financial attractiveness of various strategies for a business.

Break-even analysis allows a business to understand what the minimum level of sales needed is to ensure that it does not make a loss, and how sensitive the break-even point is to changes in fixed or variable expenses. It can help you to understand and examine the profit drivers of your business.

HOW IT WORKS IN PRACTICE

Say you are an entrepreneur looking to sell t-shirts across Europe. You will want to know how many t-shirts you need to sell before your venture generates a profit. This figure can then be compared to your sales forecasts to judge the likely success of your venture. There are two ways of calculating break-even points, as shown below.

The variable cost of producing a single t-shirt is $1. The fixed costs of the business over a year (those costs that won't vary month to month) include items such as telecommunications, rent, and insurance, and total $25,000 in year one. The unit price you are expecting for each t-shirt is $5 and your projected sales in year one are 50,000 units.

To calculate break-even, either draw a chart showing:

- sales revenue at different levels of output;
- fixed costs at different levels of output;
- total costs at different levels of output.

The point where total cost equals total sales revenue is the break-even point.

Or use the data available to calculate the contribution of each unit sold or made. This is the difference between the sales revenue and the variable cost of each unit. Using the example of the t-shirts, each t-shirt brings in $5 of revenue against $1 in variable costs. The contribution of each unit is said to be $4, because the unit makes a $4 contribution towards fixed costs.

The number of units needed to be sold to break even is therefore the total fixed cost divided by the contribution per unit. The t-shirt venture would need to sell enough t-shirts to cover fixed costs ($25,000) divided by the unit contribution ($4)—in other words, 6,250 shirts.

Break-even analysis is particularly useful in comparing alternative scenarios. For example, you might consider what happens if labor costs rise and the variable cost of producing a t-shirt doubles to $2. In this scenario, the contribution per shirt falls to $3 but fixed costs remain $25,000—meaning the business now needs to sell 25,000 ÷ 3 t-shirts to reach break-even (8,334 shirts).

The simple formula for this method is:

$$\text{Break-even sales (\$)} = \frac{\text{Fixed costs}}{\left(\dfrac{\text{Contribution margin}}{\text{Total sales}}\right)}$$

TRICKS OF THE TRADE

- Fundamentally, there are only three ways to reduce break-even: lower direct costs to increase the gross margin; reduce fixed expenses and lower necessary total costs; or raise prices to increase revenues.
- Categorizing costs as fixed or variable is essential for break-even analysis. Fixed costs are those not related to the volume of production, often referred to as "overheads." These costs will remain static even if you do not produce any goods, and include items such as staff salaries, insurance, property taxes, and interest. Variable costs are those related to production output or

sales, and might include raw materials, commission, packaging, and shipping costs. Without a good understanding of your costs, break-even analysis will be meaningless.

- Remember that the break-even point is not a static figure. You should compare projections to real-life results every three to six months, and make adjustments if necessary. In particular, expenses tend to increase over time and you may fall below break-even point because you think it is lower than it has become.
- When conducting break-even analysis, you might want to add in a margin for profit. For example, you might want to target a specific profit margin goal and this can be incorporated into break-even analysis as follows:

$$\text{Break-even (\$)} = \frac{(\text{Fixed costs} + \text{Profit goal})}{\left(\frac{\text{Contribution margin}}{\text{Total sales}}\right)}$$

- Another refinement of the break-even analysis is the "sensitivity analysis." This refers to using the break-even point to evaluate different scenarios. For example, what happens if you increase prices by 25%? What happens if unit sales fall by 20%? Using a spreadsheet, it is very simple to perform such calculations quickly, allowing you to look at different situations.

MORE INFO

Articles:

"Fixed, variable costs and break-even." *The Times 100*. Online at: tinyurl.com/6eeuxkj

"Mind Your Business—Break-even analysis: Debts, revenues and costs." *Biz/ed* (November 18, 2008). Online at: www.bized.co.uk/current/mind/2008_9/181108.htm

Capital Asset Pricing Model

Although at first glance it looks likes a simple formula, the capital asset pricing model (CAPM) represents an historic effort to understand and quantify something that's not at all simple: risk. Conceived by Nobel economist William Sharpe in 1964, CAPM has been praised, appraised, and assailed by economists ever since.

WHAT IT MEASURES

The relationship between the risk and expected return of a security or stock portfolio.

WHY IT IS IMPORTANT

The capital asset pricing model's importance is twofold.

First, it serves as a model for pricing the risk in all securities, and thus helps investors evaluate and measure portfolio risk and the returns they can anticipate for taking such risks.

Second, the theory behind the formula also has fueled—some might say provoked—spirited debate among economists about the nature of investment risk itself. The CAPM attempts to describe how the market values investments with expected returns.

The CAPM theory classifies risk as being either diversifiable, which can be avoided by sound investing, or systematic, that is, not diversified and unavoidable due to the nature of the market itself. The theory contends that investors are rewarded only for assuming systematic risk, because they can mitigate diversifiable risk by building a portfolio of both risky stocks and sound ones.

One analysis has characterized the CAPM as "a theory of equilibrium" that links higher expected returns in strong markets with the greater risk of suffering heavy losses in weak markets; otherwise, no one would invest in high-risk stocks.

HOW IT WORKS IN PRACTICE

CAPM holds that the expected return of a security or a portfolio equals the rate on a risk-free security plus a risk premium. If this expected return does not meet or beat a theoretical required return, the investment should not be undertaken. The formula used to create CAPM is:

Expected return = Risk-free rate + (Market return – Risk-free rate) × Beta value

The risk-free rate is the quoted rate on an asset that has virtually no risk. In practice, it is the rate quoted for 90-day US Treasury bills. The market return is the percentage return expected of the overall market, typically a published index such as Standard & Poor's. The beta value is a figure that measures the volatility of a security or portfolio of securities compared with the market as a whole. A beta of 1, for example, indicates that a security's price will move with the market. A beta greater than 1 indicates higher volatility, while a beta less than 1 indicates less volatility.

Say, for instance, that the current risk-free rate is 4%, and the S&P 500 index is expected to return 11% next year. An investment club is interested in determining next year's return for XYZ Software Inc., a prospective investment. The club has determined that the company's beta value is 1.8. The overall stock market always has a beta of 1, so XYZ Software's beta of 1.8 signals that it is a riskier investment than the overall market represents. This added risk means that the club should expect a higher rate of return than the 11% for the S&P 500. The CAPM calculation, then, would be:

$$4\% + (11\% - 4\%) \times 1.8 = 16.6\%$$

What the results tell the club is that given the risk, XYZ Software Inc. has a required rate of return of 16.6%, or the minimum return that an investment in XYZ should generate. If the investment club doesn't think that XYZ will produce that kind of return, it should probably consider investing in a different company.

TRICKS OF THE TRADE

- As experts warn, CAPM is only a simple calculation built on historical data of market and stock prices. It does not express anything about the company whose stock is being analyzed. For example, renowned investor Warren Buffett has pointed out that if a company making Barbie™ dolls has the same beta as one making pet rocks, CAPM holds that one investment is as good as the other. Clearly, this is a risky tenet.

- While high returns might be received from stocks with high beta shares, there is no guarantee that their respective CAPM return will be realized (a reason why beta is defined as a "measure of risk" rather than an "indication of high return").
- The beta parameter itself is historical data and may not reflect future results. The data for beta values are typically gathered over several years, and experts recommend that only long-term investors should rely on the CAPM formula.
- Over longer periods of time, high-beta shares tend to be the worst performers during market declines.

MORE INFO

Article:

Burton, Jonathan. "Revisiting the capital asset pricing model." *Dow Jones Asset Manager* (May/June 1998): 20–28. Online at: www.stanford.edu/~wfsharpe/art/djam/djam.htm

Website:

Contingency Analysis resource for trading, financial engineering, and financial risk management: www.contingencyanalysis.com

See Also:

Expected Rate of Return (pp. 141–142)

Capital Expenditure

WHAT IT MEASURES

Capital expenditure (capex) refers to the money a business spends purchasing or upgrading fixed assets for future business benefit. Capital expenditure can include money spent for new property that will be resold, or which might be kept for one or more years. Capital expenditure also includes money spent to improve property (or inventory) that you already own. Under international reporting standards, property is considered to be improved only if the money you spend increases or restores an item's value, prolongs its useful life, or enables the item to be used for a new purpose.

WHY IT IS IMPORTANT

Understanding capital expenditure is a vital part of assessing a company's free cash flow. Basically, if a company spends a lot on capital expenditure but doesn't show a corresponding rate of growth, it is considered a less attractive investment. Ideally, healthy companies should generate enough positive cash flow to fund dividends/growth as well as capital expenditure.

HOW IT WORKS IN PRACTICE

To enable cash flow to be properly assessed it is important to calculate accurately the amount of funds necessary to support capital expenditure—and for the business to continue to operate. This is known as capex per share.

First, you should discount any capital expenditure that is discretionary—such as real estate, which might otherwise be leased.

Then use the following formulas to calculate capex per share based on net cash outflow attributable to property, divided by the weighted average number of ordinary shares in issue during the year:

Capital expenditure = Total asset purchases − Property asset purchases − Nonproperty asset sales and

$$\text{Capex per share} = \frac{\text{Capex}}{\text{Weighted average of shares in issue}}$$

TRICKS OF THE TRADE

- Remember that few companies have smooth capex investment over time. Most companies will have a lean capex year, followed by a year or two of heavy investment. Wherever possible, use an average capex calculation—a single figure can be extremely misleading.
- Capital expenditure is only used to refer to one-off purchases of new items or improvements to existing assets which are kept and used by the business. So the cost of buying a truck for your business is a capital expenditure, but the cost of hiring a truck is not.
- It is possible to claim tax relief on a percentage of most capital expenditure, using allowances such as "first year allowance" or "writing down allowance."
- One classic example of capital expenditure is the start-up expenses incurred when you buy or create a new business venture. These expenses are considered capital expenditure because the owner incurs them to acquire property that will be kept. These expenses may be fully deducted in year one, or may be amortized over several years.

MORE INFO

Website:

HMRC (UK) Business Income Manual section on capex: www.hmrc.gov.uk/manuals/bimmanual/BIM35000.htm

Capitalization Ratios

Capitalization ratios, also widely known as financial leverage ratios, provide a glimpse of a company's long-term stability and ability to withstand losses and business downturns.

WHAT THEY MEASURE

By comparing debt to total capitalization, these ratios reflect the extent to which a corporation is trading on its equity, and the degree to which it finances operations with debt.

While not the focus here, capitalization ratio also refers to the percentage of a company's total capitalization contributed by debt, preferred stock, common stock, and other equity.

WHY THEY ARE IMPORTANT

By itself, any financial ratio is a rather useless piece of information. Collectively, and in context, though, financial leverage ratios present analysts and investors with an excellent picture of a company's situation, how much financial risk it has taken on, its dependence on debt, and developing trends. Knowing who controls a company's capital tells one who truly controls the enterprise!

HOW THEY WORK IN PRACTICE

A business finances its assets with either equity or debt. Financing with debt involves risk, since debt legally obligates a company to pay off the debt, plus the interest the debt incurs. Equity financing, on the other hand, does not obligate the company to pay anything. It pays investors dividends—but this is at the discretion of the board of directors. To be sure, business risk accompanies the operation of any enterprise. But how that enterprise opts to finance its operations—how it blends debt with equity—may heighten this risk.

Various experts include numerous formulas among capitalization financial leverage ratios. Three are discussed separately: debt-to-capital ratio, debt-to-equity ratio, and interest coverage ratios.

What's known as the capitalization ratio *per se* can be expressed in two ways:

$$\frac{\text{Long-term debt}}{(\text{Long-term debt} + \text{Owners' equity})}$$

and

$$\frac{\text{Total debt}}{(\text{Total debt} + \text{Preferred and common equity})}$$

For example, a company whose long-term debt totals $5,000 and whose owners hold equity worth $3,000 would have a capitalization ratio of:

$$\frac{5{,}000}{(5{,}000 + 3{,}000)} = \frac{5{,}000}{8{,}000} = 0.625$$

Both expressions of the capitalization ratio are also referred to "component percentages," since they compare a company's debt with either its total capital (debt plus equity) or its equity capital. They readily indicate how reliant a company is on debt financing.

TRICKS OF THE TRADE

- Capitalization ratios need to be evaluated over time, and compared with other data and standards. A gross profit margin of 20%, for instance, is meaningless—until one knows that the average profit margin for an industry is 10%; at that point, 20% looks quite attractive. Moreover, if the historical trend of that margin has been climbing for the last three years, it strongly suggests that a company's management has sound and effective policies and strategies in place.
- Also, all capitalization ratios should be interpreted in the context of a company's earnings and cash flow, and those of its competitors.

- Take care in comparing companies in different industries or sectors. The same figures that appear to be low in one industry can be very high in another.
- Some less frequently used capitalization ratios are based on formulas that use the book value of equity (the stock). When compared with other ratios, they can be misleading, because there usually is little relation between a company's book value and its market value—which is apt to be many times higher, since market value reflects what the investment community thinks the company is worth.

MORE INFO

Book:

Walsh, Ciaran. *Key Management Ratios*. 4th ed. London: FT Prentice Hall, 2008.

See Also:

Debt/Capital Ratio (pp. 98–99)
Debt/Equity Ratio (pp. 100–102)
Interest Coverage (pp. 158–159)

Central Limit Theorem

WHAT IT MEASURES

The central limit theorem (CLT) is a statistical theory which holds that, given a sufficiently large sample size from a sufficiently varied population, the mean of all results will be approximately equal to the mean of the population. In addition, samples will roughly follow a normal distribution pattern (i.e., a bell-shaped curve), with variances reflecting the variance of the source population, divided by the sample size. As a rule of thumb, a population sample of 50 is required for CLT to be applied.

WHY IT IS IMPORTANT

CLT is a relatively simple analytical tool that is very important in examining returns from a particular investment. CLT is the foundation for many statistical procedures, including quality control charts, because the distribution of the phenomenon under study does not have to be normal, because the average will be.

HOW IT WORKS IN PRACTICE

CLT states that the average of the sum of a large number of independent, identically distributed random variables with finite means and variances converges to a normal random variable.

For example, if you tossed an ordinary coin 100 times, you would expect sometimes the coin to land on heads, sometimes on tails. If you score one point for each time it lands heads, the result would be the sum of 100 independent, identically distributed random variables.

The central limit theorem states that the distribution of heads will be close to a normal distribution curve. Repeating the experiment more times would create a result that, when plotted on a graph, would closely resemble the normal curve. CLT theory is based on the idea that a large population of independent variables (like the toss of a coin) is subject to independent random effects, which result in a normal distribution.

Expressed as a mathematical formula, CLT is as follows:

Let X_1, X_2, …, X_n be a random sample (independent and identically distributed) from a distribution with well-defined and finite mean (μ_X) and variance (σ^2_X).

As n increases, the sampling distribution of the sample average and the total sum approach Normal distributions with corresponding means and variances.

TRICKS OF THE TRADE

- A very loose form of CLT says that if you add up a large number n of different random variables, and if none of those variables dominate the resultant distribution spread, the sum will eventually look Normal as n gets bigger.
- The CLT almost always holds, but you must be cautious when using it. If the population mean doesn't exist, then CLT is not applicable. Moreover, even if the mean does exist, the CLT convergence to a normal density might be slow, requiring hundreds or even thousands of observations, rather than the few dozen in these examples.

MORE INFO

Websites:

iSixSigma on CLT: tinyurl.com/3mk6we6

Richard Lowry on CLT: vassarstats.net/central.html

Contribution Margin

Finding the contribution margin unearths an important comparison that otherwise would lie hidden in an income statement.

WHAT IT MEASURES

The amounts that individual products or services ultimately contribute to net profit.

WHY IT IS IMPORTANT

Contribution margin helps a business to decide how it should direct or redirect its resources.

When managers know the contribution margin—or margins, as is more often the case—they can make better decisions about adding or subtracting product lines, investing in existing products, pricing products or services (particularly in response to competitors' actions), structuring sales commissions and bonuses, where to direct marketing and advertising expenditures, and where to apply individual talents and expertise.

In short, contribution margin is a valuable decision-support tool.

HOW IT WORKS IN PRACTICE

Its calculation is straightforward:

Contribution margin = Sales price − Variable cost

Or, for providers of services:

Contribution margin = Total revenue − Total variable cost

For example, if the sales price of a good is $500 and the variable cost is $350, the contribution margin is $150, or 30% of the sales price.

This means that 30 cents of every sales dollar remains to contribute to fixed costs and to profit after the costs directly related to the sales are subtracted.

Contribution margin is especially useful to a company comparing different products or services (see the example below).

	Product A	Product B	Product C
Sales price	$260	$220	$140
Variable costs	$178	$148	$65
Contribution margin	$82	$72	$75
Contribution margin	31.5%	32.7%	53.6%

Obviously, Product C has the highest contribution percentage, even though Product A generates more total profit. The analysis suggests that the company might do well to aim to achieve a sales mix with a higher proportion of Product C. It further suggests that prices for Products A and B may be too low, or that their cost structures need attention. Notably, none of this information appears on a standard income statement.

Contribution margin can also be tracked over a long period of time using data from several years of income statements. It can also be invaluable in calculating volume discounts for preferred customers, and break-even sales or volume levels.

TRICKS OF THE TRADE

Contribution margin depends on accurately accounting for all variable costs, including shipping and delivery, or the indirect costs of services. Activity-based cost accounting systems aid this kind of analysis. Variable costs include all direct costs (usually labor and materials). Contribution margin analysis is only one tool to use. It will not show so-called loss leaders, for example. And it doesn't consider marketing factors like existing penetration levels, opportunities, or mature markets being eroded by emerging markets.

MORE INFO

See Also:

Break-Even Analysis (pp. 48–50)
Marginal Cost (pp. 169–170)

Conversion Price

As often as not, when you need to calculate conversion price, it is not so much the calculation that is at issue, but observation.

WHAT IT MEASURES

The price per share at which the holder of convertible bonds, or debentures, or preferred stock, can convert them into shares of common stock.

Depending on specific terms, the conversion price may be set when the convertible asset is issued.

WHY IT IS IMPORTANT

The conversion price is a key factor in an investment strategy. Knowing it helps investors to determine whether or not it is to their advantage to convert their holdings into shares of stock, sell them on the open market, or retain them until they mature or are called by the issuing company.

At the same time, existing stockholders of the issuing company need to know the point at which the value of their shares could be diluted by the creation of additional shares without the concurrent creation of additional capital.

For companies themselves, a conversion price represents an additional financing option: an opportunity to convert debt into equity, an action that itself has advantages and drawbacks.

HOW IT WORKS IN PRACTICE

If the conversion price is set, it will appear in the indenture, a legal agreement between the issuer of a convertible asset and the holder, which states specific terms. If the conversion price does not appear in the agreement, a conversion ratio is used to calculate the conversion price.

A conversion ratio of 25:1, for example, means that 25 shares of stock can be obtained in exchange for each $1,000 of convertible asset held. In turn, the conversion price can be determined simply by dividing $1,000 by 25:

$$\frac{1{,}000}{25} = \$40 \text{ per share}$$

Comparison of a stock's conversion price to its prevailing market price can help to decide the best course of action. If the stock of the company in question is trading at $52 per share, converting makes sense because it increases the value of $1,000 convertible to $1,300 ($52 × 25 shares). But if the stock is trading at $32 per share, then the conversion value is only $800 ($32 × 25), and it is clearly better to defer conversion.

TRICKS OF THE TRADE

- Conversion ratios may change over time according to the terms of the agreement. This is to ensure that a convertible asset holder is not unduly advantaged and that the value of existing stock is not diluted—which, of course, would anger existing stockholders.
- Stockholders, in turn, need to monitor closely a company that decides to issue a large number of convertible assets, since the value of their shares could ultimately be undermined.
- Convertible bonds closely follow the price of the issuing company's underlying stock. Often, in fact, the respective prices of the bond and the shares to be exchanged are almost equal.

MORE INFO

See Also:

Conversion Ratio (pp. 65–66)
Convertible Preferred Stock (pp. 67–72)

Conversion Ratio

Conversion ratio and conversion price work in tandem and should be considered together.

WHAT IT MEASURES

The number of shares of common stock an investor will receive on converting a convertible security—a bond, debenture, or preferred stock.

The conversion price may be set when the convertible security is issued, depending on its terms.

WHY IT IS IMPORTANT

Like conversion price, the conversion ratio is an investment strategy tool which is used to determine what the value of a convertible security would be if it were converted immediately. By knowing a convertible's value, an investor can compare it with the prevailing price of the issuing company's common stock and decide whether it is best to convert or to continue holding the convertible.

By the same token, holders of common stock in the company issuing the convertible can use the conversion ratio to help to monitor the value of their stock. For example, a relatively high ratio could mean that the value of their shares would be diluted if large numbers of convertible holders were to exercise their options.

HOW IT WORKS IN PRACTICE

In the same way as conversion price, the conversion ratio may be established when the convertible is issued. If that is the case, the ratio will appear in the indenture, the binding agreement that details the convertible's terms.

If the conversion ratio is not set, it can be calculated quickly: divide the par value of the convertible security (typically $1,000) by its conversion price:

$$\frac{\$1{,}000}{\$40 \text{ per share}} = 25 \text{ shares}$$

In this example, the conversion ratio is 25:1, which means that every bond held with a $1,000 par value can be exchanged for 25 shares of common stock.

Knowing the conversion ratio enables an investor to decide quickly whether his convertibles (or group of them) are more valuable than the shares of common stock they represent. If the stock is currently trading at $30, the conversion value is $750, or $250 less than the par value of the convertible. It would therefore be unwise to convert.

TRICKS OF THE TRADE

- Although it is rare, a convertible's indenture can sometimes contain a provision stating that the conversion ratio will change over the years.
- A conversion ratio that is set when a convertible is issued usually protects against any dilution from stock splits. However, it does not protect against a company issuing secondary offerings of common stock.
- "Forced conversion" means that the company can make holders convert into stock at virtually any time. Convertible holders should also pay close attention to the price at which the bonds are callable.
- Conversion ratio also describes the number of shares of one common stock to be issued for each outstanding share of another common stock when a merger takes place.

MORE INFO

See Also:

Conversion Price (pp. 63–64)
Convertible Preferred Stock (pp. 67–72)

Convertible Preferred Stock

Convertible preferred stock (known as preference shares in the United Kingdom) gives the holder the right to exchange it at a fixed price for another security, usually common stock. The trick is knowing if, and when, to exercise that right.

GETTING STARTED

- Evaluating convertible preferred stock is principally an analysis of risk rather than of a company.
- Preferred stocks are listed as equity on a balance sheet, but they perform more like bonds than common stock since most of these issues pay a fixed dividend set at the time of issue.
- While holders of preferred stock are entitled to a fixed dividend, they do not usually have voting rights.
- Preferred stocks are usually repayable at par value, and rank above the claims of ordinary stockholders but behind bank and trade creditors.
- An expensive form of capitalization, preferred stock is typically used to finance growth opportunities and capital expenditures, and to repay bank debt and nonbank short-term debt.
- Preferred stocks are often preferred by venture capitalists because they protect their investments better, and offer them greater leverage and growth opportunities.
- US income tax considerations severely limit the appeal of preferred stock among individual investors, but enhance it among corporations.

FAQS

Officially, what is convertible preferred stock?

It is a share of corporation ownership that gives holders a claim on earnings prior to the claim of common stockholders and, generally, on assets in the event of liquidation. It may also be exchanged for a fixed number of shares of common stock. Because no maturity date is stipulated, preferred stock is priced based on a stated dividend yield—in, for example, dollars, pounds, or euros—or as a percentage of par value.

How does preferred stock compare to common stock?

The dividend on common stock is uncertain and variable: high when a company performs well, low or nonexistent when it fares poorly. Holders of preferred stock, however, get a fixed dividend—and one which, if not paid, accrues until it can be. On the other hand, preferred stockholders are not usually able to vote on pertinent resolutions unless dividends fall into arrears, while holders of common stock have voting rights based on the number of shares owned.

Are there different kinds of preferred stock?

Yes. For example, callable preferred stock may be repurchased by the issuing company, typically at par value or slightly higher, while an indirect convertible may be exchanged for another convertible security, such as a bond that can be exchanged for convertible preferred stock. There are also participating preferred stocks, which entitle holders both to receive specified dividends and to participate along with holders of common stock in receiving additional dividends.

Any there other important distinguishing features of preferred stock?

First, there may be an option to receive cash for those who decline to exercise their conversion rights. Most preferred stocks also carry lower interest rates than similar fixed-interest securities, since the investor has the opportunity to convert his holdings to common stock and, in turn, to realize a capital gain if its price rises above its conversion price. Some preferred stocks also permit the investor to require the issuing company to redeem the stock after a predetermined time for an amount that gives the investor a modest profit.

Venture capitalists are known to prefer preferred stock. Why?

It gives them preference in the event of a company's liquidation or sale, which enables venture capitalists to get back their investment before other investors receive any proceeds from such events. A typical convertible preferred stock also enables venture capitalist investors to convert their shares into common stock according to a predetermined formula and to vote on major stockholder issues such as the election of directors and a change of the company's core business activity.

How are repeated conversions of preferred stock prevented from diluting the value of common stock?

The formula used to convert the convertible preferred stock into shares of common stock typically includes an adjustment mechanism—an "anti-dilution provision"—that protects the investor against any dilution in his percentage ownership caused by sale of cheaper stock to later investors. The nature and extent of the protection afforded can be very important also to the holders of the company's common stock: the greater the protection against dilution given to the holder of convertible preferred stock, the more dilution common stockholders are likely to suffer

MAKING IT HAPPEN

Like almost any stock consideration, evaluating convertible preferred stock opportunities and transactions is based on research, market knowledge, and past experience.

It is essential first to understand what a company does and how it generates cash. The next question is determining the likelihood of the company being able to pay its preferred dividends. The tools of choice are, first, a common "coverage ratio" like EBIT or EBITDA, and, second, preferred stock ratings.

EBITDA is the acronym for "earnings before interest, taxes, depreciation, and amortization." It usually measures a company's ability to handle debt service (interest payments), but can easily be adapted to include preferred stock dividends. The ratio is:

$$\frac{\text{EBITDA}}{(\text{Interest expense} + \text{Preferred dividends})}$$

The higher the coverage ratio, the better.

Like corporate bonds, most preferred stocks are rated by such services as Standard & Poor's and Moody's. Each rating service uses a slightly different rating system, but they have a similar basis: "A" is good, "AAA" is better, and so on. A "B" or above is considered investment grade, but anything below that is regarded as very high risk.

Another warning point is that, if a preferred stock is rated only by one of the second-tier rating agencies, the likelihood is that the company's management was unable to get a favorable rating from Standard & Poor's or Moody's. The investor relations offices and websites of most corporations will provide the ratings. If they do not, beware—although the websites of the rating services themselves will probably list them.

There are also some guidelines to follow. For instance, preferred stocks should have a higher yield than the issuing company's comparable debt (yield is the annual dividend divided by the price). This must be gauged on a case-by-case basis.

There is another long-held contention that higher-quality companies issue standard convertible preferred stock, while lower-quality companies issue convertible exchangeable preferred stock. Similarly, it is maintained that only the "best" companies are consistently able to issue straight debt cost-effectively, while medium-quality companies issue convertible securities, and lower-quality companies or high-risk companies tend to issue additional common stock.

Conversion ratios and prices are other key facts to know about preferred stock. This information is found on the indenture statement that accompanies all issues. Occasionally the indenture will state that the conversion ratio will change over time. For example, the conversion price might be $50 for the first five years, $55 for the next five years, and so forth. Stock splits can affect conversion considerations.

In theory, convertible preferred stocks (and convertible exchangeable preferred stocks) are usually perpetual in time. However, issuers tend to force conversion or induce voluntary conversion for convertible preferred stock within 10 years. Steadily increasing common stock dividends is one inducement tactic used.

As a result, the conversion feature for preferred stocks often resembles that of debt securities. Call protection for the investor is usually about three years, and a 30- to 60-day call notice is typical.

About 50% of convertible equity issues also have a "soft call provision." If the common stock price reaches a specified ratio, the issuer is permitted to force conversion before the end of the normal protection period. Converting preferred stock risks diluting common stock, of course, and among mature companies that is a valid concern. Where a company has a good track record and aggressive growth plans, however, it may benefit both investors and the company, especially if the management can maintain (or increase) profit margin.

TRICKS OF THE TRADE

- In any country, tax considerations invariably accompany the exercise of convertible preferred stock transactions. Here are considerations based on US laws:
- Like common stock, preferred stock comes with a prospectus that should answer such basic questions as: Are the dividends cumulative? Are the shares redeemable; if so, when? What is the likelihood of redemption? Has the board of directors ever suspended dividends? (If it has, this is a bad sign indicating cash flow problems).
- At least in the United States, many companies dislike issuing preferred stock because it is an expensive form of capitalization. Preferred stock pays dividends from after-tax profits, while bonds pay interest from pre-tax dollars, thus delivering a tax break that preferred stock cannot match.
- Owning preferred stocks of other companies is another matter, however: corporations are exempt from taxes on up to 80% of preferred dividend income.
- Missing preferred stock dividends is not legally a default, but a company that omits a preferred stock dividend may not pay common stock dividends. Moreover, if subsequent preferred stock dividends are missed, preferred stock shareholders may

gain board seats (or more of them), and in some cases also accrue special voting rights.

- Most preferred issues are cumulative, so dividends accrue even if they are not actually paid in a given quarter. Once the dividends are resumed, and before common dividends can be paid, cumulative preferred shareholders must be paid their accrued dividends.
- If a company is liquidated, holders of preferred stock are entitled to receive their investment back before the holders of any common stock receive anything. In other words, "investment" means the amount paid for the preferred stock plus any accrued and unpaid dividends—an important consideration.
- Preferred stocks and other convertible securities offer investors a hedge: fixed-interest income without sacrificing the chance to participate in a company's capital appreciation.
- When a company does well, investors can convert their holdings into common stock that is more valuable. When a company is less successful, they can still receive interest and principal payments, and also recover their investment and preserve their capital if a more favorable investment appears.

MORE INFO

Book:

Jenks, Philip, and Stephen Eckett. *The Global Investor Book of Investing Rules*. London: Harriman House, 2001.

See Also:

Conversion Price (pp. 63–64)
Conversion Ratio (pp. 65–66)

Cost of Goods Sold

WHAT IT MEASURES

For a retailer, cost of goods sold (COGS) is the cost of buying and acquiring the goods that it sells to its customers. For a service company, COGS is the cost of the employee services it supplies. For a manufacturer, COGS is the cost of buying the raw materials and manufacturing its finished products.

WHY IT IS IMPORTANT

Cost of goods sold may help a company to determine the prices to charge for its products and services, and the volume of business that it needs to maintain in order to operate profitably.

For retailers especially, the cost of the merchandise sold is typically the largest expense, and thus is an absolutely critical business factor. However, understanding COGS is an important success factor for any business because it can reveal opportunities to reduce costs and improve operations.

COGS is also a key figure on an income statement, and an important consideration in computing income taxes because of its close relationship to inventory, which tax authorities treat as future income.

HOW IT WORKS IN PRACTICE

Essentially, COGS is equal to a company's opening inventory of goods and services, plus the cost of goods bought and direct costs incurred during a particular period, minus the closing inventory of goods and services.

A critical consideration is the accounting policy that a company adopts to calculate inventory values, especially if raw materials prices change during the year. This may happen often, particularly when inflation is high. Inventory values under a first in first out (FIFO) policy reflect original or older prices of materials, while a last in first out (LIFO) policy reflects current (and often more expensive) prices. Somebody computing COGS first needs to know which policy is being used, because this will affect inventory values.

COGS for a manufacturer will include a variety of items, such as raw materials and energy used in production, labor, benefits for production workers, the cost of raw materials in inventory, shipping fees, the cost of storing finished products, depreciation on production machinery used, and factory overhead expenses.

For a retail company such as Wal-Mart, COGS is generally less complex: the total amount paid to suppliers for the products being sold on its shelves.

COGS is calculated as follows:

Inventory at beginning of period	$20,000
Purchases during period	+ $60,000
Cost of goods available for sale	=$80,000
Less inventory at period end	− $15,000
Cost of goods sold (COGS)	=$65,000

Because the counting of inventory is an exhaustive undertaking for retailers, doing it quarterly or monthly would be open to error. Accordingly, tax authorities allow them to estimate cost of goods sold during the year.

Determining these estimates requires details of the gross profit margin (retailers typically use the preceding year's figure). This figure is then used to calculate the cost ratio.

Begin by assuming that net sales are 100%, then subtract the gross profit margin, say 40%, to produce a cost ratio of 60%: 100% – 40% = 60%. A monthly COGS calculation then looks like this:

Inventory at beginning of month	$10,000
Purchases during month	+ $25,000
Cost of goods available for sale	= $35,000
Less net sales during month	− $28,000
Cost ratio 100% – 40%	= 60%
Estimated cost of goods sold	= $16,800 ($28,000 × 60%)

There is another example to review, because calculating COGS for manufacturers requires additional factors:

Inventory at beginning of year	$20,000
Purchases during year	+ $50,000
Cost of direct labor	+ $15,000
Materials and supplies	+ $12,000
Misc. costs	+ $3,000
Total product expenses	= $100,000
Less inventory at year end	− $15,000
Cost of goods sold (COGS)	= $85,000

TRICKS OF THE TRADE

- Anyone who wants to determine COGS must maintain inventory and know its value!
- Because goods returned affect inventory values and, in turn, cost of goods sold, returns of goods must be reflected in COGS calculations.
- Merchandising companies may use different inventory accounting systems, but the choice has no bearing on the actual costs incurred; it only affects allocation of costs.
- COGS should not include indirect costs like administration and marketing costs, or other activities that cannot be directly attributed to producing or acquiring the product.

Covariance

WHAT IT MEASURES

Covariance measures the relationship between two random variables. For example, we might measure whether a sample population liked drinking wine, and whether they liked eating cheese. Covariance is a form of probability theory that allows us to measure the extent to which those two random variables change together. It's important to remember this does not imply causality—simply because one variable increases along with another does not mean there is necessarily a link between the two variables.

If the two variables tend to change together—showing that people who particularly enjoy drinking wine tend to particularly enjoy eating cheese—there is said to be positive covariance. If the two variables move in opposite directions—people who drink wine tend to be less keen on cheese—the covariance is said to be negative. Random variables that do not relate in either way are said to be uncorrelated.

WHY IT IS IMPORTANT

For investors, covariance is an important way of seeing how one variable is related to another, particularly when analyzing the performance of stocks or investments within a portfolio.

For example, an investor might want to see the impact that multiple changes on a portfolio affect overall returns, or the relationship between a company's debt/equity ratio and working capital cycle. Covariance is often used in measuring the performance of securities.

As a rule of thumb, a high rate of covariance suggests a portfolio that is not diversified, and which presents a high level of risk. For example, if two stock prices tend to rise and fall at the same time, these stocks would not deliver the best diversified earnings.

HOW IT WORKS IN PRACTICE

Covariance provides a way of measuring the strength of correlation between two random variables. The covariance for two random variables x and y, with a sample size of n, is as follows:

$$\text{Covariance } xy = \frac{\sum xx}{n}$$

As an example, imagine we asked four men to rate their liking for both cheese and wine, on a scale of 1 to 10. The results were as follows:

	Cheese (x)	*Wine (y)*	x	y	zy
A	3	4	–1	–2	2
B	1	4	–3	–2	6
C	3	8	–1	2	–2
D	9	8	5	2	10
Sum	16	24	0	0	16
Mean	4	6	0	0	4

To calculate the covariance, we calculate a mean for both variables. Next, both variables are transformed into deviation scores by subtracting the mean from the relevant score. The products of these deviation scores can then be calculated, summed, and averaged. The result is known as the coefficient of covariance, in this case 4.

Expressed in simpler terms: the sum of the product of variables x and y is 112, and the mean is 28. Subtracting the product of the separate means (28 – 4 × 6 yields the coefficient of covariance equal to 4).

TRICKS OF THE TRADE

- In probability theory, covariance is closely related to the concept of correlation—both of these tools are ways of measuring the similarity of two random variables.
- The coefficient of covariance has no upper or lower limits. Some statisticians point out this indeterminacy is its main disadvantage as compared with the coefficient of correlation.

- In our example, we have calculated covariance by multiplying the correlation of two random variables by the standard deviation. However, you can also calculate covariance by looking at "return surprises" (deviations from an expected return), which can be useful when analyzing securities.

Creating a Balance Sheet

WHAT IT MEASURES

The financial standing, or even the net worth or owners' equity, of a company at a given point in time, typically at the end of a calendar or fiscal year.

WHY IT IS IMPORTANT

The balance sheet shows what is owned (assets), what is owed (liabilities), and what is left (owners' equity). It provides a concise snapshot of a company's financial position.

HOW IT WORKS IN PRACTICE

However they are presented, assets must be in balance with liabilities and stockholders' equity. In other words, assets must equal liabilities plus owners' equity.

Assets include cash in hand and cash anticipated (receivables), inventory of supplies and materials, properties, facilities, equipment, and whatever else the company uses to conduct its business. Assets also need to reflect depreciation in the value of equipment, such as machinery, that has a limited expected useful life.

Liabilities include pending payments to suppliers and creditors, outstanding current and long-term debts, taxes, interest payments, and other unpaid expenses that the company has incurred.

Subtracting the value of aggregate liabilities from the value of aggregate assets reveals the value of owners' equity. Ideally, this should be positive. Owners' equity consists of capital invested by owners over the years and profits (net income) or internally generated capital, which is referred to as "retained earnings;" these are funds to be used in future operations. An example is given opposite.

Assets	*$*
Current	
Cash	8,200
Securities	5,000
Receivables	4,500
Inventory and supplies	6,300
Fixed	
Land	10,000
Structures	90,000
Equipment (less depreciation)	5,000
Intangibles/other	
...	...
Total assets	129,000

Liabilities	*$*
Payables	7,000
Taxes	4,000
Miscellaneous	3,000
Bonds and notes	25,000
Total liabilities	**39,000**
Stockholders' equity (stock, par value × shares outstanding)	80,000
Retained earnings	10,000
Total liabilities and stockholders' equity	**129,000**

TRICKS OF THE TRADE

- The balance sheet does not show a company's market worth, nor important intangibles such as the knowledge and talents of individual people, nor other vital business factors such as customers or market share.
- The balance sheet does not express the true value of some fixed assets. A six-year-old manufacturing plant, for example, is listed at its original cost, even though the price of replacing it could be much higher or substantially lower (because of new technology that might be less expensive or vastly more efficient).

- The balance sheet is not an indicator of past or future performance or trends that affect performance. It needs to be studied along with two other key reports: the income tax return and the cash flow statement. A published balance sheet needs to include prior period comparatives.

MORE INFO

Website:

Conetic Software Systems Inc.: www.conetic.com

Creating a Cash Flow Statement

WHAT IT MEASURES

Cash inflows and cash outflows over a specific period of time, typically a year.

WHY IT IS IMPORTANT

Cash flow is a key indicator of financial health, and it demonstrates to investors, creditors, and other core constituencies a company's ability to meet obligations, finance opportunities, and generally "come up with the cash" as needs arise. Cash flow that is wildly inconsistent with, say, net income, often indicates operating or managerial problems.

HOW IT WORKS IN PRACTICE

In its basic form, a cash flow statement will probably be familiar to anyone who has been a member of a club that collects and spends money. It reports funds on hand at the beginning of a given period, funds received, funds spent, and funds remaining at the end of the period.

That formula still applies to a business today, even if creating a cash flow document is significantly more complex. Cash flows are divided into three categories: cash from operations; cash investment activities; and cash financing activities. Companies with holdings in foreign currencies use a fourth category: effects of changes in exchange rates on cash.

A standard direct cash flow statement is shown opposite.

CRD, Inc. statement of cash flows for year ended December 31, 20__

	$
Cash flows from operations ($)	
Operating profit	82,000
Adjustments to net earnings	
Depreciation	17,000
Accounts receivable	−20,000

Accounts payable	12,000
Inventory	– 8,000
Other adjustments to earnings	4,000
Net cash flow from operations	*87,000*
Cash flows from investment activities ($)	
Purchases of marketable securities	– 58,000
Receipts from sales of marketable securities	45,000
Loans made to borrowers	– 16,000
Collections on loans	11,000
Purchases of plant and real estate assets	– 150,000
Receipts from sales of plant and real estate assets	47,000
Net cash flow from investment activities	*– 121,000*
Cash flows from financing activities ($)	
Proceeds from short-term borrowings	51,000
Payments to settle short-term debts	– 61,000
Proceeds from issuing bonds payable	100,000
Proceeds from issuing capital stock	80,000
Dividends paid	– 64,000
Net cash flow from financing activities	*106,000*
Net change in cash during period	**72,000**
Cash and cash equivalents, beginning of year	27,000
Cash and cash equivalents, end of year	**99,000**

TRICKS OF THE TRADE

- A cash flow statement does *not* measure net income, nor does it measure working capital.
- A cash flow statement does not include outstanding accounts receivable, but it does include the preceding year's accounts receivable (assuming these were collected during the year for which the statement is prepared).
- Add to a cash inflow any amounts charged off for depreciation, depletion, and amortization, because cash was actually spent.
- Cash equivalents are short-term, highly liquid investments, although precise definitions may vary slightly by country. These should be included when recalculating the movement of cash in the period.

- There are alternative ways to present cash flow from operations. Some texts, for example, omit earnings and adjustments, and list instead cash and interest received, cash and interest paid, and taxes received.

MORE INFO

Website:

International Accounting Standards Consultancy (IASC): www.iasc.co.uk

Creating a Profit and Loss (P&L) Account

WHAT IT MEASURES

A company's sales revenues and expenses over a period, providing a calculation of profits or losses during that time.

WHY IT IS IMPORTANT

Reading a P&L is the easiest way to tell if a business has made a profit or a loss during a given month or year. The most important figure it contains is net profit: what is left over after revenues are used to pay expenses and taxes.

Companies typically issue P&L reports monthly. It is customary for the reports to include year-to-date figures, as well as corresponding year-earlier figures to allow for comparisons and analysis.

HOW IT WORKS IN PRACTICE

A P&L adheres to a simple rule of thumb: "Revenue minus cost equals profit."

There are two P&L formats, multiple-step and single-step. Both follow a standard set of rules known as "generally accepted accounting principles" (GAAP). These rules generally adhere to requirements established by governments to track receipts, expenses, and profits for tax purposes. They also allow the financial reports of two different companies to be compared. Note that in the United Kingdom and several other nations, sales, revenues, and receipts may all be designated as turnover.

The multiple-step format is much more common, because it includes a larger number of details and is thus more useful. It deducts costs from revenues in a series of steps, allowing for closer analysis. Revenues appear first, then expenses, each in as much detail as management desires. Sales may be broken down by product line or location, while expenses such as salaries may be broken down into base salaries and commissions.

Expenses are then subtracted from revenues to show profit (or loss). A basic multiple-step P&L is shown opposite.

Multiple-step profit and loss accounts ($)

NET SALES			750,000
Less: cost of goods sold			450,000
Gross profit			300,000
LESS: OPERATING EXPENSES			
Selling expenses			
Salaries & commissions	54,000		
Advertising	37,500		
Delivery/transportation	12,000		
Depreciation/store equipment	7,500		
Other selling expenses	5,000		
Total selling expenses		116,000	
General & administrative expenses			
Administrative/office salaries	74,000		
Utilities	2,500		
Depreciation/structure	2,400		
Misc. other expenses	3,100		
Total general & admin expenses		82,000	
Total operating expenses			198,000
OPERATING INCOME			102,000
LESS (ADD): NONOPERATING ITEMS			
Interest expenses	11,000		
Interest income earned	−2,800		8,200
Income before taxes			93,800
Income taxes			32,360
Net income			**61,440**

TRICKS OF THE TRADE

- A P&L does not show how a business has earned or spent its money.
- One month's P&L can be misleading, especially if a business generates most of its receipts in particular months. A retail establishment, for example, usually generates a large percentage

of its sales in the final three months of the year, while a consulting service might generate the lion's share of its revenues in as few as two months, and no revenues at all in some other months.

- Invariably, figures for both revenues and expenses reflect the judgments of the companies reporting them. Accounting methods can be quite arbitrary when it comes to such factors as depreciation expenses.

Creditor and Debtor Days

These financial measures are two sides of the same coin, since they respectively measure the flow of money out of and into a business. As such, they are reliable indicators of both efficiency and problems.

WHAT THEY MEASURE

Creditor days is a measure of the number of days on average that a company requires to pay its creditors, while debtor days is a measure of the number of days on average that it takes a company to receive payment for what it sells. It is also called accounts receivable days.

WHY THEY ARE IMPORTANT

Creditor days is an indication of a company's creditworthiness in the eyes of its suppliers and creditors, since it shows how long they are willing to wait for payment. Within reason, the higher the number the better because all companies want to conserve cash. At the same time, a company that is especially slow to pay its bills (100 or more days, for example) may be a company having trouble generating cash, or one trying to finance its operations with its suppliers' funds. Ultimately, companies whose creditor days soar have trouble obtaining supplies.

Debtor days is an indication of a company's efficiency in collecting monies owed. In this case, obviously, the lower the number the better. An especially high number is a telltale sign of inefficiency or worse. It may indicate bad debts, dubious sales figures, or a company being bullied by large customers out to improve their own cash position at another company's expense. Customers whose credit terms are abused also risk higher borrowing costs and related charges.

Changes in both measures are easy to spot, and easy to understand.

HOW THEY WORK IN PRACTICE

To determine creditor days, divide the cumulative amount of unpaid suppliers' bills (also called trade creditors) by sales, then multiply by 365. So the formula is:

$$\text{Creditor days} = \frac{\text{Trade creditors}}{\text{Sales}} \times 365$$

For example, if suppliers' bills total $800,000 and sales are $9,000,000, the calculation is:

$$\frac{800{,}000}{9{,}000{,}000} \times 365 = 32.44 \text{ days}$$

The company takes 32.44 days on average to pay its bills.

To determine debtor days, divide the cumulative amount of accounts receivable by sales, then multiply by 365. For example, if accounts receivable total $600,000 and sales are $9,000,000, the calculation is:

$$\frac{600{,}000}{9{,}000{,}000} \times 365 = 24.33 \text{ days}$$

The company takes 24.33 days on average to collect its debts.

TRICKS OF THE TRADE

- Cash businesses, including most retailers, should have a much lower debtor days figure than noncash businesses, since they receive payment when they sell the goods. A typical target for noncash businesses is 40–50 days.
- An abnormally high creditor days figure may not only suggest a cash crisis, but also the management's difficulty in maintaining revolving credit agreements.
- An increasing number of debtor days also suggests overly generous credit terms (to bolster sales) or problems with product quality.

Current Price of a Bond

WHAT IT MEASURES

The narrow range within which a given bond price falls, based on that bond's current asking price and bid price.

WHY IT IS IMPORTANT

Current prices of comparable bonds are strong indicators of a bond's buying or selling price. Changes in bond prices are also indicators of economic strength and direction.

HOW IT WORKS IN PRACTICE

The price of a bond depends on several factors.

- Interest rates: As rates rise, a bond's price falls, because it pays less interest than current offerings and is thus less attractive. Conversely, a bond becomes more attractive as interest rates fall.
- The risk perceived for the issuing entity, reflected in its credit rating from one of the major rating agencies. The price of a bond of a company in bankruptcy, for instance, will be low because the company may never be able to redeem it. The price of a bond from a strong company may include a premium over its face or "par" value because it is considered a reliable investment: a bond with a face value of $1,000 might sell for $1,050, indicating a $50 premium.
- The issuing of new bonds by corporations or other bodies (and the ratings they receive) affects the prices of existing bonds.

Daily bond tables vary in format, but list the basic information necessary for comparing prices. Only a small fraction of the outstanding bonds trade on any given day, but these representative prices provide sufficient information to estimate what a fair price would be for the bonds being considered.

When considering bonds, several pieces of information are essential:

- the bond's coupon rate—what it will pay in interest;
- how long before the principal amount of the bond matures, or if there is a call date;

- its recent price and current yield.

Essentially, all the tables provide this basic information. The US Treasury table, for example, would be listed as follows:

Rate	Maturity	Bid	Ask	Yield
$7\frac{3}{4}$	Feb 2012	105:12	105:14	5.50
$5\frac{3}{8}$	Feb 2012	99:26	99:27	5.44

In the first row, the security is paying its bondholders $7\frac{3}{4}$% interest and is due to mature in February 2012. Prices in the bid and ask columns are percentages of the bond's face value of $1,000. A bid of 105:12 means that a buyer was willing to pay $1053.75, compared to the seller's lowest asking price, 105:14, or $1054.38, a difference of 63 cents per thousand.

Bond quotes follow certain conventions. Prices are given as percentages of face value, but the digits appearing after the colons are not decimals, being expressed in terms of 1/32. So 12/32, for example, would equal $3.75, which is appended to the 105 before the colon: $1053.75.

The bid and ask prices indicate that an investor who bought the bond at par when it was first issued can make a profit of more than 5% if it were sold now. The last column gives the yield to maturity, an interest rate summarizing the bond's overall investment value.

COMMON MISTAKES

- A bond's yield and its price are not the same. Price is what is paid for a bond; yield expresses the percentage return on the investment. Yield is most useful for comparing fixed-income investments for planning purposes, rather than as an exact measure of the return expected from an investment.
- The number of bond issues outstanding at any given time is far greater than stocks, and most bondholders buy with the intent of holding them until maturity, so the amount of trading is limited.
- There are several bond-rating agencies. A bond's rating indicates its level of risk.
- Listing tables also show the volume traded along with the current yield.

- The internet offers many calculators for quickly determining bond prices and yields.

MORE INFO

Article:

Kamlet, Art, and Chris Lott. "Bonds—Basics." *The Investment FAQ* (July 5, 1998). Online at: www.invest-faq.com/articles/bonds-a-basics.html

Website:

InvestingInBonds.com, from the Securities Industry and Financial Markets Association (SIFMA): www.investinginbonds.com

See Also:

Bond Yield (pp. 38–40)

Current Ratio

The current ratio is a key liquidity ratio and a staple for anyone who borrows or lends money.

WHAT IT MEASURES

A company's liquidity and its ability to meet its short-term debt obligations.

WHY IT IS IMPORTANT

By comparing a company's current assets with its current liabilities, the current ratio reflects its ability to pay its upcoming bills in the unlikely event of all creditors demanding payment at once. It has long been the measurement of choice among financial institutions and lenders.

HOW IT WORKS IN PRACTICE

The current ratio formula is simply:

$$\text{Current ratio} = \frac{\text{Current assets}}{\text{Current liabilities}}$$

Current assets are the ones that a company can turn into cash within 12 months during the ordinary course of business. Current liabilities are bills due to be paid within the coming 12 months.

For example, if a company's current assets are $300,000 and its current liabilities are $200,000, its current ratio would be:

$$\frac{300{,}000}{200{,}000} = 1.5$$

As a rule of thumb, the 1.5 figure means that a company should be able to get hold of $1.50 for every $1.00 it owes.

TRICKS OF THE TRADE

- The higher the ratio, the more liquid the company. Prospective lenders expect a positive current ratio, often of at least 1.5. However, too high a ratio is cause for alarm, because it indicates declining receivables and/or inventory—signs that portend declining liquidity.
- A current ratio of less than 1 suggests pressing liquidity problems, specifically an inability to generate sufficient cash to meet upcoming demands.
- Managements use current ratio as well as lenders; a low ratio, for example, may indicate the need to refinance a portion of short-term debt with long-term debt to improve a company's liquidity.
- Ratios vary by industry, however, and should be used accordingly. Some sectors, such as supermarket chains and restaurants, perform nicely with low ratios that would keep others awake at night.
- One shortcoming of the current ratio is that it does not differentiate assets, some of which may not be easily converted to cash. As a result, lenders also refer to the quick ratio.
- Another shortcoming of the current ratio is that it reflects conditions at a single point in time, such as when the balance sheet is prepared. It is possible to make this figure look good just for this occasion: lenders should not, therefore, appraise these conditions by the ratio alone.
- A constant current ratio and falling quick ratio signal trouble ahead, because this suggests that a company is amassing assets at the expense of receivables and cash.

MORE INFO

See Also:

Acid-Test Ratio (pp. 7–9)
Liquidity Ratio Analysis (pp. 163–165)

Days Sales Outstanding

Days sales outstanding (DSO) can be considered as a tool for financial troubleshooters.

WHAT IT MEASURES

A company's average collection period, or the average number of days it takes a company to convert its accounts receivable into cash. Commonly referred to as DSO, it is also called the collection ratio.

WHY IT IS IMPORTANT

Knowing how long it takes a company to turn accounts receivable into cash is an important financial indicator. It indicates the efficiency of the company's internal collection, suggests how well a company's customers are accepting its credit terms (net 30 days, for example), and is a figure that is routinely compared with industry averages.

Ideally, DSOs should be decreasing or constant. A low figure means the company collects its outstanding receivables quickly. Typically, DSO is reviewed quarterly or yearly (91 or 365 days).

DSO also helps to expose companies that try to disguise weak sales. Large increases in DSO suggest that a company is trying to force sales either by accepting poor receivable terms or selling products at discount to book more sales for a particular period. An improving DSO suggests that a company is striving to make its operations more efficient.

Any company with a significant change in its DSO merits examination in greater detail.

HOW IT WORKS IN PRACTICE

Regular DSO requires three figures: total accounts receivable, total credit sales for the period analyzed, and the number of days in the period (annual, 365; six months, 182; quarter, 91). The formula is:

$$\text{Days sales outstanding} = \frac{\text{Accounts receivable}}{\text{Total credit sales for the period}} \times \text{Number of days in the period}$$

For example: if total receivables are $4,500,000, total credit sales in a quarter are $9,000,000, and number of days is 91, then:

$$\frac{4{,}500{,}000}{9{,}000{,}000} \times 91 = 45.5 \text{ days}$$

Thus, it takes an average of 45.5 days to collect receivables.

TRICKS OF THE TRADE

- Companies use DSO information with an accounts receivable aging report. This lists four categories of receivables: 0–30 days, 30–60 days, 60–90 days, and over 90 days. The report also shows the percentage of total accounts receivable that each group represents, allowing for an analysis of delinquencies and potential bad debts—a figure that appears on a profit and loss account.
- A rarely used related calculation, best possible DSO, shows how long it takes a company to collect current receivables. Its formula is:

$$\text{Best possible DSO} = \frac{\text{Current receivables}}{\text{Total credit sales for the period}} \times \text{Number of days in the period}$$

So, current receivables of $3,000,000 and total credit sales of $9,000,000 in a 91-day period would result in a best possible DSO of 30.3 days (3,000,000 ÷ 9,000,000 × 91).

- Only credit sales of merchandise should be used in calculating DSO; cash sales are excluded, as are sales of such items as fixtures, equipment, or real estate.
- Properly evaluating an acceptable DSO requires a standard for comparison. A traditional rule of thumb is that DSO should not

exceed one-third to one-half of selling terms. For instance, if terms are 30 days, acceptable DSO would be 40 to 45 days.

- A single DSO is only a snapshot. A fuller picture would require at least quarterly calculations, and some companies review DSO monthly.
- DSO can vary widely by industry as well as company. For example, clothing wholesalers have to have the goods on retailers' shelves for months before they will be sold and the retailer is able to cover invoices. However, a computer wholesaler with a lengthy DSO suggests trouble, since computers become obsolete quickly.

MORE INFO

See Also:

Asset Utilization (pp. 29–31)

Debt/Capital Ratio

Whether called debt/capital ratio, debt-to-capital ratio, or simply debt ratio, this is a fundamental tool in analyzing how a company is funded. It is also known as the gearing ratio.

WHAT IT MEASURES

The percentage of total funding represented by debt.

WHY IT IS IMPORTANT

By comparing a company's long-term liabilities to its total capital, the debt/capital ratio provides a review of the extent to which a company relies on external debt financing for its funding and is a measure of the risk to its stockholders.

The debt/capital ratio is also a measure of a company's borrowing capacity, and of its ability to pay scheduled financial payments on term debts and capital leases. Bond-rating agencies and analysts use it routinely to assess creditworthiness. The greater the debt, the higher the risk.

However, it can be misleading to assume that the lowest ratio is automatically the best ratio. A company may assume large amounts of debt in order to expand the business. Utilities, for instance, have high capital requirements, so their debt/capital ratios will be high as a matter of course. So are those of manufacturing companies, especially those developing a new technology or new product.

At the same time, the higher the level of debt, the more important it is for a company to have positive earnings and steady cash flow.

HOW IT WORKS IN PRACTICE

Although there are variations on exactly what goes into this ratio, the most common method is to divide total long-term debt by total assets (total long-term debt plus stockholders' funds), or:

$$\text{Debt/capital ratio} = \frac{\text{Total liabilities}}{\text{Total assets}}$$

For example, if the balance sheet of a corporate annual report lists total liabilities of $9,800,000 and total stockholders' equity of $12,800,000, the debt/capital ratio is (calculating in thousands):

$$\frac{9{,}800}{(9{,}800 + 12{,}800)} = \frac{9{,}800}{22{,}600}$$
$$= 0.434$$
$$= 43.4\%$$

Some formulas distinguish different portions of long-term debt. However, that complicates calculations and many experts regard it as unnecessary. It is also common to express the formula as total debt divided by total funds, which produces the same outcome.

TRICKS OF THE TRADE

- If a company has minority interests in subsidiaries that are consolidated in the balance sheet, they must be added to stockholders' equity.
- Debt calculations should include capital leases.
- One rule of thumb holds that a debt/capital ratio of 60% or less is acceptable, but another holds that 40% is the most desirable.
- A high debt/capital ratio means less security for stockholders, because in bankruptcies debt holders are paid first. It still can be tolerable, however, if a company's return on assets exceeds the rate of interest paid to creditors.
- Do not confuse the debt/capital ratio with debt/capitalization, which compares debt with total market capitalization and fluctuates as the company's stock price changes.

MORE INFO

See Also:

Capitalization Ratios (pp. 56–58)
Debt/Equity Ratio (pp. 100–102)

Debt/Equity Ratio

Debt/equity is the most commonly used method of assessing corporate debt, but in fact there is more than one way of expressing essentially the same thing.

WHAT IT MEASURES

How much money a company owes compared with how much money it has invested in it by principal owners and stockholders.

WHY IT IS IMPORTANT

The debt/equity ratio reveals the proportion of debt and equity a company is using to finance its business. It also measures a company's borrowing capacity. The higher the ratio, the greater the proportion of debt—but also the greater the risk.

Some even describe the debt/equity ratio as "a great financial test" of long-term corporate health, because debt establishes a commitment to repay money throughout a period of time, even though there is no assurance that sufficient cash will be generated to meet that commitment.

Creditors and lenders, understandably, rely heavily on the ratio to evaluate borrowers.

HOW IT WORKS IN PRACTICE

The debt/equity ratio is calculated by dividing debt by owners' equity, where equity is, typically, the figure stated for the preceding calendar or fiscal year. Debt, however, can be defined either as long-term debt only, or as total liabilities, which include both long- and short-term debt.

The most common formula for the ratio is:

$$\text{Debt/equity ratio} = \frac{\text{Total liabilities}}{\text{Owners' equity}}$$

In our example, a company's long-term debt is $8,000,000, its short-term debt is $4,000,000, and owners' equity totals

$9,000,000. The debt/equity ratio would therefore be (calculating in thousands):

$$\frac{(8{,}000 + 4{,}000)}{9{,}000} = \frac{12{,}000}{9{,}000} = 1.33$$

An alternative debt/equity formula considers only long-term liabilities in the equation. Accordingly:

$$\frac{8{,}000}{9{,}000} = 0.889$$

There is also a third method, which is the reciprocal of the debt-to-capital ratio; its formula is:

$$\text{Debt/equity ratio} = \frac{\text{Owners' equity}}{\text{Total funds}}$$

However, this would be more accurately defined as "equity/debt ratio."

TRICKS OF THE TRADE

- It is important to understand exactly how debt is defined in the ratio presented.
- When calculating the ratio, some prefer to use the market value of debt and equity rather than the book value, since book value often understates current value.
- For this ratio, a low number indicates better financial stability than a high one does; if the ratio is high, a company could be at risk, especially if interest rates are rising.
- A ratio greater than one means assets are mainly financed with debt; less than one means equity provides most of the financing. Since a higher ratio generally means that a company has been aggressive in financing its growth with debt, volatile earnings can result owing to the additional cost of interest.
- Debt/equity ratio is somewhat industry-specific, and often depends on the amount of capital investment required.

MORE INFO

See Also:

Capital Expenditure (pp. 54–55)
Debt/Capital Ratio (pp. 98–99)

Defining Assets

WHAT THEY MEASURE

Collectively, the value of all the resources a company uses to conduct business and generate profits. Examples of assets are cash, marketable securities, accounts and notes receivable, inventory of merchandise, real estate, machinery and office equipment, natural resources, and intangibles such as patents, legal claims and agreements, and negotiated rights.

WHY THEY ARE IMPORTANT

No business can continue for very long without knowing what assets it has at its disposal, and using them efficiently. Assets are a reflection of organizational strength, and are invariably evaluated by potential investors, banks, and creditors, and other stakeholders. Moreover, the value of assets is also a key figure that is used to calculate several financial ratios.

HOW THEY WORK IN PRACTICE

Assets are typically broken down into five different categories:

1. **Current assets**. These include cash, cash equivalents, marketable securities, inventory, and prepaid expenses that are expected to be used within one year or a normal operating cycle. All cash items and inventory are reported at historical value. Securities are reported at market value.
2. **Noncurrent assets**, or long-term investments. These are resources that are expected to be held for more than one year. They are reported at the lower of cost and current market value, which means that their values will vary.
3. **Fixed assets**. These include property, plant and facilities, and equipment used to conduct business. These items are reported at their original value, even though current values might well be much higher.
4. **Intangible assets**. These include legal claims, patents, franchise rights, and accounts receivable. These values can be more difficult to determine. Accounts receivable, for example,

reflect the amount a business expects to collect, such as $9,000 of the $10,000 owed by customers.

5 **Deferred charges**. These include prepaid costs and other expenditures that will produce future revenue or benefits.

TRICKS OF THE TRADE

- Assets do not necessarily include everything of value, such as the talents of individuals, an organization's collective expertise, or the value of a customer base.
- Classic definitions of assets also often exclude or undervalue trademarks, even though there is universal agreement that these— for example, the three-point star of Mercedes-Benz or Coca-Cola's red logo—can have enormous value.
- Fixed assets are valued at their original cost, because of the prevailing opinion that they are used for business and are not for sale. Moreover, current market value is essentially a matter of opinion.
- Determining the value of patents can be challenging, because a patent has a finite life span, its value declines each year, and its useful life may be even shorter.
- Some experts contend that the principal assets of "knowledge-based" businesses such as consulting firms or real estate development companies are, in fact, its people. In turn, their aggregate value should be calculated by subtracting the net value of assets from market value.

Depreciation

GETTING STARTED

Depreciation is a basic expense of doing business, reducing a company's earnings while increasing its cash flow. It affects three key financial statements: balance sheet; cash flow; and income (or profit and loss). It is based on two key facts: the purchase price of the items or property in question, and their "useful life."

Depreciation values and practices are governed by the tax laws of both national governments, and state or provincial governments, which must be monitored continuously for any changes that are made. Accounting bodies, too, have developed standard practices and procedures for conducting depreciation.

Depreciating a single asset is not difficult: The challenge lies in depreciating the many assets possessed by even small companies, and it is intensified by the impact that depreciation has on income and cash flow statements, and on income statements. It is essential to depreciate with care and to rely on experts, ensuring that they fully understand the current government rules and regulations.

FAQS

What is depreciation?

It is an allocation of the cost of an asset over a period of time for accounting and tax purposes. Depreciation is charged against earnings, on the basis that the use of capital assets is a legitimate cost of doing business. Depreciation is also a noncash expense that is added into net income to determine cash flow in a given accounting period.

What is straight-line depreciation?

One of the two principal depreciation methods, it is based on the assumption that an asset loses an equal amount of its value each year of its useful life. Straight-line depreciation deducts an equal amount from a company's earnings each year throughout the life of the asset.

What is accelerated depreciation?

The other principal method of depreciation is based on the assumption that an asset loses a larger amount of its value in the early years of its useful life. Also known as the "declining-balance" method, it is used by accountants to reduce a company's tax bills as soon as possible, and is calculated on the basis of the same percentage rate each year of an asset's useful life. Accelerated depreciation better reflects the economic value of the asset being depreciated, which tends to become increasingly less efficient and more costly to maintain as it grows older.

What can be depreciated?

To qualify for depreciation, assets must:

- be used in the business;
- be items that wear out, become obsolete, or lose value over time from natural causes or circumstances;
- have a useful life beyond a single tax year.

Examples include vehicles, machines and equipment, computers and office furnishings, and buildings, plus major additions or improvements to such assets. Some intangible assets can also be included under certain conditions.

What cannot be depreciated?

Land, personal assets, inventory, leased or rented property, and a company's employees.

MAKING IT HAPPEN

In order to determine the annual depreciation cost of assets, it is necessary first to know the initial cost of those assets, how many years they will retain some value for the business, and what value, if any, they will have at the end of their useful life.

For example, a company buys a truck to carry materials and finished goods. The vehicle loses value as soon as it is purchased, and then loses more with each year it is in service, until the cost of repairs exceeds its overall value. Measuring the loss in the value of the truck is depreciation.

Straight-line depreciation is the most straightforward method, and is still quite common. It assumes that the net cost of an asset should be written off in equal amounts over its life. The formula used is:

$$\frac{\text{Original cost} - \text{Scrap value}}{\text{Useful life}}$$

For example, if the truck cost $30,000 and can be expected to serve the business for 7 years, its original cost less its scrap value would be divided by its useful life:

$$\frac{(30{,}000 - 2{,}000)}{7} = \$4{,}000 \text{ per year}$$

The $4,000 becomes a depreciation expense that is reported on the company's year-end income statement under "operation expenses."

In theory, an asset should be depreciated over the actual number of years that it will be used, according to its actual drop in value each year. At the end of each year, all the depreciation claimed to date is subtracted from its cost in order to arrive at its "book value," which would equal its market value. At the end of its useful business life, any undepreciated portion would represent the salvage value for which it could be sold or scrapped.

For tax purposes, some accountants prefer to use accelerated depreciation to record larger amounts of depreciation in the asset's early years in order to reduce tax bills as soon as possible. In contrast to the straight-line method, the accelerated or declining balance method assumes that the asset depreciates more in its earlier years of use. The table compares the depreciation amounts that would be available, under these two methods, for a $1,000 asset that is expected to be used for five years and then sold for $100 in scrap.

	Straight-line Method		Declining-balance Method	
Year	Annual Depreciation	Year-end Book Value	Annual Depreciation	Year-end Book Value
1	\$900 × 20 per cent = \$180	\$1,000 – \$180 = \$820	\$1,000 × 40 per cent = \$400	\$1,000 – \$400 = \$600
2	\$900 × 20 per cent = \$180	\$820 – \$180 = \$640	\$600 × 40 per cent = \$240	\$600 – \$240 = \$360
3	\$900 × 20 per cent = \$180	\$640 – \$180 = \$460	\$360 × 40 per cent = \$144	\$360 – \$144 = \$216
4	\$900 × 20 per cent = \$180	\$460 – \$180 = \$280	\$216 × 40 per cent = \$86.40	\$216 – \$86.40 = \$129.60
5	\$900 × 20 per cent = \$180	\$280 – \$180 = \$100	\$129.60 × 40 per cent = \$51.84	\$129.60 – \$51.84 = \$77.76

While the straight-line method results in the same deduction each year, the declining-balance method produces larger deductions in the first years and far smaller deductions in the later years. One result of this system is that, if the equipment is expected to be sold for a higher value at some point in the middle of its life, the declining-balance method can produce a greater taxable gain in that year because the book value of the asset will be relatively lower.

The depreciation method to be used for a particular asset is fixed at the time that the asset is first placed in service. Whatever rules or tables are in effect for that year must be followed as long as the asset is owned.

Depreciation laws and regulations change frequently over the years as a result of government policy changes, so a company owning property over a long period may have to use several different depreciation methods.

TRICKS OF THE TRADE

- With very specific exceptions, it is not possible to deduct in one year the entire cost of an asset if that asset has a useful life substantially beyond the tax year.
- To qualify for depreciation, an asset must be put into service. Simply purchasing it is not enough. There are rules that govern how much depreciation can be claimed on items put into service after a year has begun.
- It is common knowledge that if a company claims more depreciation than it is entitled to, it is liable for stiff penalties in a tax audit, just as failure to allow for depreciation causes an overestimation of income. What is not commonly known is that if a company does not claim all the depreciation deductions it is entitled to, it will be considered as having claimed them when taxable gains or losses are eventually calculated on the sale or disposal of the asset in question.
- While leased property cannot be depreciated, the cost of making permanent improvements to leased property can be (remodeling a leased office, for example). There are many rules governing leased assets; they should be depreciated with care.

- Another common mistake is to continue depreciating property beyond the end of its recovery period. Cars are common examples of this.
- Conservative companies depreciate many assets as quickly as possible, despite the fact that this practice reduces reported net income. Knowledgeable investors watch carefully for such practices.

MORE INFO

Book:

Wolf, Frank K., and W. Chester Finch. *Depreciation Systems*. Ames, IA: Iowa State University Press, 1994.

Websites:

Bankrate.com on Section 179 of the United States Internal Revenue Code: tinyurl.com/y4lc

Business Owner's Toolkit: www.bizfilings.com/toolkit/

See Also:

Residual Value (pp. 218–220)

Discounted Cash Flow

WHAT IT MEASURES

Discounted cash flow (DCF) is a way of measuring the net present value (NPV) of future cash flow. This allows companies to express the value of an investment today based on predicted future returns. The idea behind discounted cash flow is that $1 today is worth more than $1 you might receive in the future. The money you have now can be invested and might generate interest whereas money you haven't yet received can't be used in this way, and there is a risk it might not be received. Therefore, discounted cash flow is a way of adjusting the value of future money over time to reflect its "real" value today.

WHY IT IS IMPORTANT

Discounted cash flow is most useful when future operating conditions and cash flow are variable, or where trading conditions are expected to change significantly over time. It is a good way of assessing the likely value of money the business will receive in future, and therefore DCF is considered one of the best ways of valuing an investment.

HOW IT WORKS IN PRACTICE

To calculate discounted cash flow, you must first determine the forecasted cash flow of a company, and choose a discount rate based on the expected or desired rate of return. The discount rate chosen should reflect the risk that the return will not be achieved—a higher risk should result in a higher discount rate.

Next, use the discount rate for each year to discount cash flow to the "correct" adjusted present value, as shown in the example below. Remember, cash flow will lose value over time because it is discounted for a longer period.

For example:

$$\text{NPV} = \frac{\text{CF1}}{(1+r)} + \frac{\text{CF2}}{(1+r)^2} + \frac{\text{CF3}}{(1+r)^3}$$

where NPV is the net present value of cash flows, CF1, CF2, and CF3 are predicted cash flows in years 1, 2, and 3, respectively, and *r* is the discount rate. It's worth remembering that, unless the series of cash flows has a known finite endpoint, a terminal value will need to be assumed.

TRICKS OF THE TRADE

- Cash flows may represent interest payments or repayments, or in the case of stocks can relate to dividends.
- There are many variations to the calculation illustrated above, and different ways to measure cash flow and discount rates in a DCF calculation. All the different approaches are basically ways of estimating the return from an investment, adjusted for the time value of money.
- Like many calculations, a DCF figure is only as good as the figures used for cash flow and discount rates. Small changes in these figures can result in enormous variation in NPV figures, so it's often wiser to use DCF over a relatively short period of time and to adopt a terminal value approach, rather than discounting to infinity.
- DCF analysis of cash flow should be used when a business case deals with two potential uses of money, and wherever cash flow timing is different.

MORE INFO

Article:

McClure, Ben. "DCF analysis." *Investopedia*. Online at: www.investopedia.com/university/dcf/

Website:

Solution Matrix on DCF: www.solutionmatrix.com/discounted-cash-flow

Distinguishing between a Capital and an Operating Lease

GETTING STARTED

Determining whether a lease obligation is an operating or capital lease, for financial reporting purposes, requires that it be evaluated on the basis of four criteria established by the FASB (Financial Accounting Standards Board). The criteria are objective rules for making a judgment about who, the lessor or the lessee, bears the risks and benefits of ownership of the leased property.

If a lease is determined to be a capital lease, an asset and corresponding liability are recorded at the present value of the minimum lease payments. The capital asset is depreciated over time, while the liability is amortized as lease payments are made. Rental payments under operating leases are simply expensed as incurred. Due to the complexity of lease agreements, management judgment still plays a large role in distinguishing between operating and capital leases.

FAQS

What are minimum lease payments?

The minimum lease payments are the rental payments to be made during the lease term, plus the amount of the bargain price, guaranteed residual value, or penalty for failure to renew the lease at the end of its original term.

In determining whether a lease should be classified as an operating or capital lease, what interest rate should be used?

The interest rate used to discount the minimum lease payments to their present value is the incremental borrowing rate of the lessee, this being the interest rate that the lessee would have been charged if the assets had been acquired by borrowing the purchase price. If the lessor's implied interest rate for the lease is known and is lower than the lessee's estimated incremental borrowing rate, then the lessee uses the implied rate to discount.

MAKING IT HAPPEN

The Four FASB Criteria

Until the 1970s, many companies used leasing as a means to purchase tangible assets without recognizing their ownership or the lease obligation on the balance sheet. In substance, leases were off-balance-sheet financing. Although all leases were required to be disclosed in the footnotes to the financial statements, even long-term finance leases did not appear as a liability. Because the basic measures of leverage do not consider off-balance-sheet obligations, the accounting profession and the investment community believed that there needed to be more stringent guidelines for classifying leases as operating or financing, and in 1976 the FASB issued Statement no. 13, "Accounting for leases." The statement sets out four criteria to distinguish between an operating and a capital (finance) lease:

- The lease agreement transfers ownership of the assets to the lessee during the term of lease.
- The lessee can purchase the assets leased at a bargain price, such as $1, at the end of the lease term.
- The lease term is at least 75% of the economic life of the leased asset.
- The present value of the minimum lease payments is 90% or greater of the asset's value.

If a lease agreement does not meet any of these criteria, the lessee treats it as an operating lease for accounting purposes. If, however, the agreement meets one of the above criteria, it is treated as a capital lease.

Accounting for a Capital Lease

Capital leases are reported by the lessee as if the assets being leased were acquired and the monthly rental payments as if they were payments of principal and interest on a debt obligation. Specifically, the lessee capitalizes the lease by recognizing an asset and a liability at the lower of the present value of the minimum lease payments or the value of the assets under lease. As the monthly rental payments are made, the corresponding liability decreases. At the same time, the leased asset is depreciated in a manner that is consistent with other owned assets having the same use and economic life.

Accounting for an Operating Lease

If the lease is classified as an operating lease, the monthly lease payments are simply treated as rental expenses and recognized on the income tax return as they are incurred. There is no recognition of a leased asset or liability.

Clearing Up Remaining Confusion

The FASB's attempt to establish objective criteria for distinguishing between operating and capital leases was a good first step. This has enabled companies to make prudent financial decisions in lease versus buy situations, based on the accounting treatment afforded a specific lease structure. Furthermore, financial professionals now have a framework within which to determine what lease terms create a capital lease. However, the use of financial engineering still occurs. Consequently, many leases that are truly financing leases are recorded as operating leases, because their provisions have been altered to avoid qualification as capital leases.

When in doubt, a manager should always ask whether the risks and benefits of ownership have truly been passed from the lessor to the lessee. Facts indicating that the transfer has occurred are when maintenance, insurance, and property tax expenses are borne by the lessee, or when the lessee guarantees a specific residual value on the leased property.

MORE INFO

Websites:

Institute of Chartered Accountants in England and Wales (ICAEW): www.icaew.com

Securities and Exchange Commission (SEC; US): www.sec.gov

Dividend Yield

WHAT IT MEASURES

An investment's dividend yield is a measure of the dividend paid on stock, expressed as a percentage over one year. This measure is frequently used in stock quotes and financial reports, and is based upon the company's annual cash dividend per share and the current stock price.

WHY IT IS IMPORTANT

A stock's dividend yield is a crucial measure for potential investors in any company, since it illustrates how much cash flow is generated for each dollar invested in equity, on top of any capital gains made from a rising stock price. A relatively high-paying, stable stock will attract income investors, and the higher the dividend yield, the greater expected return for income investors. Historical data also show that stocks which pay a dividend have generally outperformed non-dividend-paying stocks in the long term.

HOW IT WORKS IN PRACTICE

To calculate a dividend yield, you will need to use the following formula:

$$\text{Dividend yield} = \frac{\text{Annual dividend per share}}{\text{Stock price per share}}$$

For example, Company A has an annual dividend per share of $10, and the average quarterly value of its stock per share is $75. To assess the company's dividend yield, we would divide the dividend by the stock price, as follows:

$$\frac{10}{75} = 0.1333 = 13.33\%$$

On this basis, the stock has a dividend yield of 13.33%.

Company B might also pay an annual dividend per share of $10, but if its stock is trading at $20 per share, then its dividend yield will be 50%—considerably higher than Company A's dividend yield. Assuming other factors are equal, income investors would find Company B a more attractive investment opportunity.

TRICKS OF THE TRADE

- Dividend yield is often simply referred to as a "yield" in financial markets.
- The dividend yield helps to explain a company's value to investors but can vary widely depending on a company's market position, industry, earnings, cash flow, and dividend policy. Therefore, this measure is not always important for long-term investors who are concerned with a company's long-term growth.
- It isn't a guarantee, but many studies show a strong correlation between yield and returns over five years—companies with higher yields tend to offer higher returns, while lower yields lead to lower returns.
- It is common for newspapers to include yield figures in tables showing stock performance and share prices. In general, a yield of around 2–4% is considered average, and most attractive to longer-term growth investors.
- High yields are generally offered by mature, well-established companies while younger companies tend to pay lower yields because they are focused on growth. Many young companies will not pay any dividend at all.
- If a company has a low yield compared to others in the same industry, this could mean the company's stock is over-valued because investors are confident of future growth. Alternatively, it can suggest that the company can't afford to pay the expected dividends.
- If a company has a high yield in comparison to others in the same sector, it could suggest imminent dividend cuts.

MORE INFO

Websites:

Biz/ed on dividend yield: www.bized.co.uk/compfact/ratios/investor8.htm

Investopedia dividend yield calculator: www.investopedia.com/calculator/DivCYield.aspx

See Also:

Earnings per Share (pp. 121–123)
Yield (pp. 275–276)

Earnings at Risk

WHAT IT MEASURES

Earnings at risk (EAR) measures the quantity by which net income might change in the event of an adverse change in interest rates. It is a risk measurement which is closely linked with value at risk (VAR) calculations. The difference is that while VAR looks at the change in the entire value over the forecast horizon, EAR looks at potential changes in cash flows or earnings.

WHY IT IS IMPORTANT

Companies engaged in international business face many risks from changing currency levels to fluctuating interest rates. The challenge for investors and financial professionals is understanding and quantifying how these risks affect the profitability of the business.

Calculating EAR helps you to understand the impact of interest rate changes on your company's financial position, but it can be a challenge to calculate as transaction volumes grow or portfolio complexity increases. For this reason, banks and large corporations will rely on specialist computer applications using the Monte Carlo method to calculate EAR.

HOW IT WORKS IN PRACTICE

There are various models available to calculate EAR, but at heart most will calculate EAR by using a variation of:

Principal amount × Interest × Time period = Interest income and interest expense

However, EAR is not this simple in reality! Most EAR models will allow you to add in numerous factors that affect interest income and expense, such as time periods for various rates received, outstanding balances, or interest rates received and paid.

In addition, the model will simulate various possible interest rate scenarios over a period of several quarters or years, to determine their potential effect on earnings. There might be dozens of projections covering short-term rates, long-term rates, risk spreads, etc, over the specified time period. For each quarter, the model will calculate income and expense based on assumed interest rates, and can be adapted to reflect hypothetical rate changes, illustrating different strategies and customer behaviors.

If most of the likely scenarios do not seriously reduce earnings, then the organization's interest rate exposure is low. If the scenarios result in unacceptable changes, the organization might consider looking at changes to its strategy.

TRICKS OF THE TRADE

- Because of the number of variables that can be applied to EAR modeling, no two models will look the same, even if applied to the same organization. It is therefore essential to ask for specific details when analyzing any EAR summary.
- A typical EAR model will show analysis for up to a 300 basis point increase or fall in interest rates. These may be shown as a single rise or fall, or gradual change in rates. The EAR will also show a "confidence interval" showing impact according to, for example, a 90% confidence interval.
- Very few organizations devise EAR models from scratch, but will rely on summary results generated by computer. However, managers may well need to analyze EAR reports generated by specialized modeling tools and applications.

MORE INFO

Book:

Lam, James. *Enterprise Risk Management: From Incentives to Controls*. Hoboken, NJ: Wiley, 2003.

Websites:

Approximity on EAR: www.approximity.com/risk/Products/cfar.html

Financial Risk Manager on EAR: tinyurl.com/6b5odvd

Earnings per Share

Earnings per share (EPS) is perhaps the most widely used ratio there is in the investing realm.

WHAT IT MEASURES

The portion of a company's profit allocated to each outstanding share of a company's common stock.

WHY IT IS IMPORTANT

Earnings per share is simply a fundamental measure of profitability that shows how much profit has been generated on a per-share-of-stock basis. Were the term worded as profit per share, the meaning certainly would be much clearer, if not self-evident.

By itself, EPS doesn't reveal a great deal. Its true value lies in comparing EPS figures across several quarters, or years, to judge the growth of a company's earnings on a per-share basis.

HOW IT WORKS IN PRACTICE

Essentially, the figure is calculated after paying taxes and dividends to preferred stockholders and bondholders. Barring extraordinary circumstances, EPS data are reported quarterly, semiannually, and annually.

To calculate EPS, start with net income (earnings) for the period in question, subtract the total value of any preferred stock dividends, then divide the resulting figure by the number of shares outstanding during that period:

$$\text{Earnings per share} = \frac{(\text{Net income} - \text{Dividends on preferred stock})}{\text{Average number of shares outstanding}}$$

By itself, this formula is simple enough. Alas, defining the factors used in the formula invariably introduces complexities and—as some allege on occasion—possible subterfuge.

For instance, while companies usually use a weighted average number of shares outstanding over the reporting period, shares outstanding can still be either "primary" or "fully diluted." Primary EPS is calculated using the number of shares that are currently held by investors in the market and able to be traded. Diluted EPS is the result of a complex calculation that determines how many shares would be outstanding if all exercisable warrants and options were converted into common shares at the end of a quarter. Suppose, for example, that a company has granted a large number of share options to employees. If these options are capable of being exercised in the near future, that could alter significantly the number of shares in issue and, thus, the EPS—even though the E part (the earnings) is the same. Often in such cases, the company might quote the EPS both on the existing shares and on the fully diluted version. Which one a person considers depends on their view of the company and how they wish to use the EPS figure. In addition, companies can report extraordinary EPS, a figure which excludes the financial impact of unusual occurrences, such as discontinued operations or the sale of a business unit.

Net income or earnings, meanwhile, can be defined in a number of ways, based on respective nations' generally accepted accounting principles.

For example, "pro-forma earnings" tend to exclude more expenses and income used to calculate "reported earnings." Pro-forma advocates insist that these earnings eliminate all distortions and present "true" earnings that allow pure apples-with-apples comparisons with preceding periods. However, "nonrecurring expenses" seem to occur with such increasing regularity that one may wonder if a company is deliberately trying to manipulate its earnings figures and present them in the best possible light, rather than in the most accurate light.

"Cash" earnings are earnings from operating cash flow—notably, not EBITDA. In turn, cash EPS is usually these earnings divided by diluted shares outstanding. This figure is very reliable because operating cash flow is not subject to as much judgment as net earnings or pro-forma earnings.

TRICKS OF THE TRADE

- Given the varieties of earnings and shares reported today, investors need to determine first what the respective figures represent before making investment decisions. There are cases of a company announcing a pro-forma EPS that differs significantly from what is reported in its financial statements. Such discrepancies, in turn, can affect how the market values a given stock.
- Investors should check to see if a company has issued more shares during a given period, since that action, too, can affect EPS. A similar problem occurs where there have been a number of shares issued during the accounting period being considered. Which number of issued shares do you use, the opening figure, the closing figure, or the mean? In practice the usual method is to use the weighted mean number of shares in issue during the year (weighted, that is, for the amount of time in the year that they were in issue).
- "Trailing" earnings per share is the sum of EPS from the last four quarters and is the figure used to compute most price-to-earnings ratios.
- Diluted and primary shares outstanding can be the same if a company has no warrants or convertible bonds outstanding, but investors should not assume anything, and need to be sure how "shares outstanding" is being defined.

MORE INFO

Article:

Wayman, Rick. "The 5 types of earnings per share." *Investopedia*. Online at: www.investopedia.com/articles/analyst/091901.asp

See Also:

Dividend Yield (pp. 116–118)
Price/Earnings Ratio (pp. 197–198)
Return on Stockholders' Equity (pp. 229–230)

EBITDA

EBITDA—an acronym that stands for "earnings before interest, taxes, depreciation, and amortization"—is slightly less inclusive than "EBIT"—earnings before interest and taxes. Both focus on profitability, and have gained popularity in the past decade as measures of operating success. But as this popularity has grown, so has the number of the measure's critics.

WHAT IT MEASURES

A company's earnings from ongoing operations, before net income is calculated.

WHY IT IS IMPORTANT

EBITDA's champions contend it gives investors a sense of how much money a young or fast-growing company is generating before it pays interest on debt, taxes, and accounts for noncash changes. If EBITDA grows over time, champions argue, investors gain at least a sense of long-term profitability and, in turn, the wisdom of their investment.

Business appraisers and investors also may study EBITDA to help to gauge a company's fair market value, often as a prelude to its acquisition by another company. It is also frequently applied to companies that have been subject to leveraged buyouts—the strategy being that EBITDA will help to cover loan payments needed to finance the transaction.

EBITDA, and EBIT, too, are claimed to be good indicators of cash flow from business operations, since they report earnings before debt payments, taxes, depreciation, and amortization charges are considered. However, that claim is challenged by many—often rather vigorously.

HOW IT WORKS IN PRACTICE

EBITDA first appeared as leveraged buyouts soared in popularity during the 1980s. It has since become well established as a financial analysis measure of telecommunications, cable, and major media companies.

Its formula is quite simple. Revenues less the cost of goods sold, general and administrative expenses, and the deductions of items expressed by the acronym EBITDA:

EBITDA = Revenue
− Expenses (excluding interest, taxes, depreciation, and amortization)

or

EBIT = Revenue − Expenses (excluding taxes and interest)

This formula does not measure true cash flow. A communications company, for example, once reported $698 million in EBIT but just $324 million in cash from operations.

TRICKS OF THE TRADE

- As yet no definition of EBITDA is enforced by standards-making bodies, so companies can all but create their own. As a result, EBITDA can easily be manipulated by aggressive accounting policies, which may erode its reliability.
- Ignoring capital expenditures could be unrealistic and horribly misleading, because companies in capital-intensive sectors such as manufacturing and transportation must continually make major capital investments to remain competitive. High-technology is another sector that may be capital-intensive, at least initially.
- Critics warn that using EBITDA as a cash flow indicator is a huge mistake, because EBITDA ignores too many factors that have an impact on true cash flow, such as working capital, debt payments, and other fixed expenses. Interest and taxes can, and do, cost a company cash, they point out, while debt holders have higher claims on a company's liquid assets than investors do.
- Critics further assail EBITDA as the barometer of choice of unprofitable firms because it can present a more optimistic view of a company's future than it has a right to claim. *Forbes*

magazine, for instance, once referred to EBIDTA as "the device of choice to pep up earnings announcements."

- Even so, EBITDA may be useful in terms of evaluating firms in the same industry with widely different capital structures, tax rates, and depreciation policies.

Economic Value Added

WHAT IT MEASURES

A company's financial performance—specifically, whether it is earning more or less than the total cost of the capital supporting it.

WHY IT IS IMPORTANT

Economic value added measures true economic profit, or the amount by which the earnings of a project, an operation, or a corporation exceed (or fall short of) the total amount of capital that was originally invested by the company's owners.

If a company is earning more, it is adding value, and that is good. If it is earning less, the company is in fact devouring value, and that is bad, because the company's owners (stockholders, for example) would be better off investing their capital elsewhere.

The concept's champions declare that EVA forces managers to focus on true wealth creation and maximizing stockholder investment. By definition, then, increasing EVA will increase a company's market value.

HOW IT WORKS IN PRACTICE

EVA is conceptually simple and easy to explain: From net operating profit, subtract an appropriate charge for the opportunity cost of all capital invested in an enterprise—the amount that could have been invested elsewhere. It is calculated using this formula:

EVA = Net operating profit less applicable taxes – Cost of capital

A company is considering building a new plant whose total weighted cost over 10 years is $80 million. If the expected annual incremental return on the new operation is $10 million, or $100 million over 10 years, then the plant's EVA would be positive, in this case $20 million:

100,000,000 – 80,000,000 = $20,000,000

An alternative but more complex formula for EVA is:

EVA = [Return on invested capital (%) – Cost of capital (%)]
× Original capital invested

TRICKS OF THE TRADE

- EVA is a measure of dollar surplus value, not the percentage difference in returns.
- Purists describe EVA as "profit the way stockholders define it." They further contend that if stockholders expect a 10% return on their investment, they "make money" only when their share of after-tax operating profits exceeds 10% of equity capital.
- An objective of EVA is to determine which business units best utilize their assets to generate returns and maximize stockholder value; it can be used to assess a company, a business unit, a single plant, an office, or even an assembly line. This same technique is equally helpful in evaluating new business opportunities.

MORE INFO

Website:

EVA at Stern Stewart & Co: www.sternstewart.com/?content=proprietary&p=eva

Efficiency and Operating Ratios

For this calculation and related ratios, the lower the numbers the better.

WHAT THEY MEASURE

The portion of operating revenues or fee income spent on overhead expenses.

WHY THEY ARE IMPORTANT

Often identified with banking and financial sectors, the efficiency ratio indicates a management's ability to keep overhead costs low. This measurement is also used by mature industries, such as steel manufacture, chemicals, or auto production, that must focus on tight cost controls to boost profitability because growth prospects are generally modest.

In some industries, the efficiency ratio is called the overhead burden, which is overheads as a percentage of sales.

A different method measures efficiency simply by tracking three other measures: accounts payable to sales, days sales outstanding, and inventory turnover, which indicates how fast a company is able to move its merchandise. A general guide is that if the first two of these measures are low and third is high, efficiency is probably high; the reverse is likewise true.

HOW THEY WORK IN PRACTICE

The efficiency ratio is defined as operating overhead expenses divided by fee income plus tax equivalent net interest income. If operating expenses are $100,000, and revenues (as defined) are $230,000, then:

$$\text{Efficiency ratio} = \frac{100{,}000}{230{,}000} = 0.43$$

However, not everyone calculates the ratio in the same way. Some institutions include all noninterest expenses, while others exclude certain charges and intangible asset amortization.

To find the inventory turnover ratio, divide total sales by total inventory. If net sales are $300,000 and inventory is $100,000, then:

$$\text{Inventory turnover ratio} = \frac{300{,}000}{140{,}000} = 2.14$$

To find the accounts payable to sales ratio, divide a company's accounts payable by its annual net sales. A high ratio suggests that a company is using its suppliers' funds as a source of cheap financing because it is not operating efficiently enough to generate its own funds. If accounts payable are $42,000 and total sales are $300,000, then:

$$\text{Accounts payable/sales ratio} = \frac{42{,}000}{300{,}000} = 0.14 = 14\%$$

TRICKS OF THE TRADE

- Identifying "overheads" to calculate the efficiency ratio can itself contribute to overall inefficiency. Some financial experts contend that efficiency can be measured equally well by reviewing earnings per share growth and return on equity.
- Some banks identify amortization of goodwill expense, and pull it out of their noninterest expense in order to calculate what is called the cash efficiency ratio: noninterest expense minus goodwill amortization expense divided into revenue.
- In banking, an acceptable efficiency ratio was once in the low 60s. Now the goal is 50, while better-performing banks boast ratios in the mid 40s. Low ratings usually indicate a higher return on equity and earnings.

Elasticity

Elasticity measures responsiveness, and is very useful when studying the impact of pricing on supply and demand.

WHAT IT MEASURES

The percentage change of one variable caused by a percentage change in another variable.

WHY IT IS IMPORTANT

Elasticity is defined as "the measure of the sensitivity of one variable to another." In practical terms, elasticity indicates the degree to which consumers respond to changes in price. It is obviously important for companies to consider such relationships when contemplating changes in price, demand, and supply.

Demand elasticity measures how much the quantity demanded changes when the price of a product or service is increased or lowered. Will demand remain constant? If not, by how much will demand change?

Supply elasticity measures the impact on supply when a price is changed. It is assumed that lowering prices will reduce supply, because demand will increase—but by how much?

HOW IT WORKS IN PRACTICE

The general formula for elasticity is:

$$\text{Elasticity} = \frac{\text{Change in } x\ (\%)}{\text{Change in } y\ (\%)}$$

In theory, *x* and *y* can be any variables. However, the most common application measures price and demand. If the price of a product is increased from \$20 to \$25, or 25%, and demand in turn falls from 6,000 to 3,000 (–50%), elasticity would be calculated as:

$$\frac{-50}{25} = -2$$

A value greater in magnitude than ±1 means that demand is strongly sensitive to price, while a lesser value means that demand is not price-sensitive.

TRICKS OF THE TRADE

- There are five cases of elasticity:
  - E = 1, or unit elasticity. The proportional change in one variable is equal to the proportional change in another variable: if price rises by 5%, demand falls by 5%.
  - E is greater than 1, or *just elastic*. The proportional change in *x* is greater than the proportional change in *y*: for example, if price rises by 5%, demand falls by 3%.
  - E = infinity, or perfectly elastic. This is a special case of elasticity: any change in *y* will effect no change in *x*. An example would be prices charged by a hospital's emergency room, where increases in price are unlikely to curb demand.
  - E is less than 1, or *just inelastic*. The proportional change in *x* is less than the proportional change in *y*: if prices are increased, say by 3%, demand will fall by 30%.
  - E = 0, or perfectly inelastic. This is another special case of elasticity: any change in *y* will have an infinite effect on *x*.
- There are more complex formulae for determining a range of variables, or "arc elasticity."
- Elasticity can be used to affirm two rules of thumb:
  - demand becomes elastic if consumers have an alternative or adequate substitute for the product or service;
  - demand is more elastic if consumers have an incentive to save money.

MORE INFO

See Also:

Price Elasticity (pp. 199–201)

Enterprise Value

In the financial world, enterprise value has a precise meaning and calculation. It is important to remember this, as many conference planners and consultants routinely rely on "enterprise value" to promote whatever concept they happen to be selling.

WHAT IT MEASURES

It measures what financial markets believe a company's ongoing operations are worth.

Some people also define enterprise value as what it would actually cost to purchase an entire company at a given moment.

WHY IT IS IMPORTANT

Enterprise value is not a theoretical valuation but a firm and finite value, logically determined. It tells an individual investor the underlying value of his stake in an enterprise. For potential acquirers considering a takeover of a company, enterprise value helps them to determine a reasonable price for their desired acquisition.

HOW IT WORKS IN PRACTICE

Although it is a finite figure, enterprise value can be calculated in two ways. One method is quicker, but the other is more thorough and thus more reliable.

The quick way is simply to multiply the number of a company's shares outstanding by the current price per share. Using this approach, the enterprise value of a company with 2 million shares outstanding, and a share price of $25, would be:

$$\text{Enterprise value} = 2{,}000{,}000 \times 25 = \$50{,}000{,}000$$

However, this value is based on the market's perception of the value of its shares of stock; it also ignores some important factors about a company's fiscal health. The second, more complete, method is therefore preferred by many experts. This method calculates enterprise value as the sum of market capitalization, plus debt and preferred stock, minus cash and cash equivalents:

$$\text{Enterprise value} = \text{Market capitalization} + \text{Long-term debt} + \text{Preferred stock} - \text{Cash and equivalents}$$

If market capitalization is $6.5 million, debt totals $1 million, the value of preferred stock is $1.5 million, and cash and equivalents total $2 million, enterprise value would be:

$$6.5 + 1 + 1.5 - 2 = \$7\text{million}$$

This more thorough calculation recognizes the existence of both a company's debt and of the amount of cash and liquid assets on hand. No matter how a stock may fluctuate, these sums are relatively constant, and the amount of debt can be very significant. Debt—and cash too—can be just as important during a company's sale, since new owners assume existing debt and receive any cash on hand. Indeed, more than a few acquisitions are financed in part with funds of the acquired company.

TRICKS OF THE TRADE

- Financial markets often use the market capitalization figure for enterprise value, but they really are not the same thing.
- Experts will occasionally refer to "total enterprise value," but its definition and formula are virtually identical to this second formula for enterprise value. Total enterprise value is only meaningful to those who use the quick method to compute enterprise value.
- A company's value is sometimes expressed as "the total funds being used to finance it." This is increasingly used in place of the price/earnings ratio, and indicates the economic rather than the accounting return that the company is generating on the total value of the capital supporting it. Companies that have borrowed heavily to finance growth, or that have paid large premiums for acquisitions or assets, are more frequently evaluated by this method.

Exchange Rate Risk

Because formulae exist to quantify, at least to a degree, the risks that accompany any investment decision, it is logical to assume that a similar formula exists to quantify what is called both exchange rate risk and currency risk. Such logic is flawed, for no such formula exists.

WHAT IT MEASURES

The risk of a gain or loss in the value of a business activity or investment that results from changes in the exchange rates of world currencies.

WHY IT IS IMPORTANT

Each business day seems to bring more international business transactions, generated by an ever-growing number of enterprises from an ever-increasing number of countries. Enterprises in developing nations, especially, are vying for their share of world commerce.

However, the economies of these developing nations can be especially fragile, while economies of mature nations periodically sputter and suffer recessions. Asia, Latin America, and Eastern Europe have all endured economic turmoil in the past decade, while such regions as the Middle East have been volatile for several decades, principally because of the wide swings in oil prices.

Currency exchange rates can be just as volatile, and this clearly poses risks to any enterprise conducting business in foreign markets and any investor holding either stock in a foreign-based company or an interest in a mutual fund that invests in foreign companies. The effects on a company's earnings, cash flow, and balance sheet can be significant.

The main exchange rate risk to an operation or investment is that any profits realized will be partially reduced—or wiped out altogether—when they are exchanged for the domestic currency, be it US dollars, pounds sterling, the euro, or Japanese yen.

More often, exchange rate risk will affect a company's price competitiveness in a product or service also offered by a competitor whose costs are incurred in a foreign currency. If the competitor's currency weakens, its relative competitive position improves because its costs decline, enabling the competitor to reduce its price and attract a larger share of a market.

HOW IT WORKS IN PRACTICE

There is a simple way to avoid the risk posed by exchange rates: don't do business abroad! For large companies, as well as an increasing number of small and medium-sized companies, that would be like sticking one's head in the sand.

A second defense against exchange rate risks is almost as unrealistic: conduct all business in your home currency. Requiring foreign customers to pay up only in, say, dollars, puts the burden of currency fluctuations squarely on the customer's shoulders and completely insulates the selling company from any shrinkage of profits from exchange rate differences. The price of such insulation, however, is likely to be a steady loss of customers.

The practical course of action, then, is to gain a basic understanding of exchange rate risks, if only enough to sort out the reams of opinions on the subject, and to select knowledgeable advisers and use their counsel wisely. This is a sophisticated, complex realm that has been examined for over a century. It is certainly no place for amateurs.

At the same time, however, exchange rates, interest rates, and inflation rates have been linked to one another via a classic set of relationships that can serve as leading indicators of changes in risk. These relationships are:

- The **Purchasing Power Parity Theory**. While it can be expressed differently, the most common expression links the changes in exchange rates to those in relative price indices in two countries:

Rate of change of exchange rate = Difference in inflation rates

- The **International Fisher Effect** (IFE). This holds that an interest rate differential will exist only if the exchange rate is expected to change in such a way that the advantage of the higher interest rate is offset by the loss on the foreign exchange transactions. Practically speaking, the IFE implies that while an investor in a low-interest country can convert funds into the currency of a high-interest country and earn a higher rate, the gain (the interest rate differential) will be offset by the expected loss due to foreign exchange rate changes. The relationship is stated as:

  Expected rate of change of the exchange rate = Interest rate differential

- The **Unbiased Forward Rate Theory**. This holds that the forward exchange rate is the best and unbiased estimate of the expected future spot exchange rate:

  Expected exchange rate = Forward exchange rate

Other than these yardsticks, defending against exchange rate risk is largely a matter of observation. In the floating exchange rate environment that has existed for almost the past 30 years, currency exchange rates respond to a host of factors: political climates, the flow of imports and exports, the flow of capital, inflation rates in various countries, consumer expectations, and confidence levels, to name a few. Frequently, limits are placed on exchange rate fluctuations by government policies—actions that themselves can arouse controversy or debate.

Even so, the exchange rate risks these factors create can be arranged into three primary categories:

- **Economic exposure**. Due to changes in rates, operating costs will rise and make a product uncompetitive in the world market, thus eroding profitability. There's little that can be done about economic risk; it's simply a routine business risk that every enterprise must endure.

- **Translation exposure**. The impact of currency exchange rates will reduce a company's earnings and weaken its balance sheet. In turn, the denominations of assets and liabilities are important, although many experts contend that currency fluctuations have no significant impact on real assets.
- **Transaction exposure**. Caused by an unfavorable move in a specific currency between the time when a contract is agreed and the time it is completed, or between the time when lending or borrowing is initiated and the time the funds are repaid. This is the most common problem that confronts most companies. Requiring payment in advance is rarely practical, and impossible, of course, for borrowing and lending.

To reduce translation exposure, experienced corporate fund managers use a variety of techniques known as currency hedging, which amounts to diversifying currency holdings, monitoring exchange rates, and acting accordingly, depending on specific conditions. Its advocates contend that taking appropriate action can greatly reduce translation risks, if not avoid them altogether. Currency hedging, however, is also technical and sophisticated.

Transaction exposure can be eased by a process known as factoring. Major exporters, in particular, transfer title to their foreign accounts receivable to a third-party factoring house that assumes responsibility for collections, administrative services, and any other services requested. The fee for this service is a percentage of the value of the receivables, anywhere from 5% to 10% or higher, depending on the currencies involved. Companies often include this percentage in selling prices to recoup the cost.

Commercial and country risks can affect exchange rates, too. Commercial risks include the default or bankruptcy of major foreign customers. While this risk mirrors what can also occur at home, foreign-based companies operate under different laws and relationships with their governments. More worrisome are country risks: political or military interventions and currency restrictions that less stable nations might impose. Insurance is available to address such risks, but it can be costly.

TRICKS OF THE TRADE

- Any number of models have been created to explain and forecast exchange rates. None has proved definitive, largely because the world's economies and financial markets are evolving so rapidly.
- A forward transaction is an agreement to buy one currency and sell another on a date some time beyond two business days. It allows an exchange rate on a given day to be locked in for a future payment or receipt, thereby eliminating exchange rate risk.
- Foreign exchange options are contracts which, for a fee, guarantee a worst-case exchange rate for the future purchase of one currency for another. Unlike a forward transaction, the option does not obligate the buyer to deliver a currency on the settlement date unless the buyer chooses to. These options protect against unfavorable currency movements while allowing retention of the ability to participate in favorable movements.
- A producer facing pricing competition caused by fluctuations in exchange rates can also use currency contracts to try to match competitors' cost structures and reduce costs.
- Companies doing larger volumes of business in a foreign country often establish a local office there to pay expenses and collect revenues in local currencies to reduce the impact of sudden and pronounced exchange rate fluctuations.
- Private sector subscription services monitor currencies and publish alerts. One US-based service has established numerical ranges that indicate risk, from 100 (no risk) to 200 (extreme risk or an outright currency crisis).
- Exchange rate risks cannot be insured against *per se*.
- The US Export-Import Bank (Eximbank) may be a source of advice for companies, especially smaller and medium-sized companies, seeking assistance.

MORE INFO

Book:

Giddy, Ian H., and Gunter Dufey. "The management of foreign exchange risk." In Frederick D. S. Choi (ed). *Handbook of International Accounting*. New York: Wiley, 1991. Also online at: www.stern.nyu.edu/~igiddy/fxrisk.htm

Article:

Magos, Alice. "Ask Alice about foreign exchange risk." *Business Owner's Toolkit*. Online at: tinyurl.com/3zdfx4z

Expected Rate of Return

Expected rate of return (ERR) is a measure conceived and crafted in the spirit of "forewarned is forearmed."

WHAT IT MEASURES

The projected percentage return on an investment, based on the weighted probability of all possible rates of return.

WHY IT IS IMPORTANT

No self-respecting businessperson or organization should make an investment without first having some understanding of how successful that investment is likely to be. Expected rate of return provides such an understanding, within certain limits.

HOW IT WORKS IN PRACTICE

The formula for expected rate of return is:

$$\text{Expected rate of return} = \sum_{i=1}^{n} [P(i) \times r_i]$$

where P(i) is the probability that the return r_i is achieved, i.e., the sum of the products of all possible returns and their probabilities.

A simple example, as given below, is far easier to grasp, and adequately illustrates the principle which the formula expresses. It will probably be of more practical use to most of those who need to calculate ERR.

The current price of ABC Inc. stock is $10. At the end of the year, ABC shares of stock are projected to be traded:

- 25% higher if economic growth exceeds expectations—a probability of 30%;
- 12% higher if economic growth equals expectations—a probability of 50%;
- 5% lower if economic growth falls short of expectations—a probability of 20%.

To find the expected rate of return, simply multiply the percentages by their respective probabilities and add the results:

$$(30\% \times 25\%) + (50\% \times 12\%) + (20\% \times -5\%) = 7.5 + 6 - 1 = 12.5\%$$

A second example:

- if economic growth remains robust (a 20% probability), investments will return 25%;
- if economic growth ebbs, but still performs adequately (a 40% probability), investments will return 15%;
- if economic growth slows significantly (a 30% probability), investments will return 5%;
- if the economy declines outright (a 10% probability), investments will return 0%.

Therefore the ERR can be calculated:

$$(20\% \times 25\%) + (40\% \times 15\%) + (30\% \times 5\%) + (10\% \times 0\%) = 5 + 6 + 1.5 + 0 = 12.5\%$$

Another method that can be used to project expected return is the capital asset pricing model (CAPM), which is explained separately.

TRICKS OF THE TRADE

- The probability totals must always equal 100% for the calculation to be valid.
- Be sure not to overlook any negative numbers in the calculations, or the results produced will be incorrect.
- An ERR calculation is only as good as the scenarios considered. Wildly unrealistic scenarios will produce an equally unreliable expected rate of return.

MORE INFO

See Also:

Capital Asset Pricing Model (pp. 51–53)
Rate of Return (pp. 207–209)

Fair Value Calculations

WHAT IT MEASURES

Fair value is the value of an asset or liability in a transaction between two parties. It can be used to refer to the complete assets and liabilities of a company that is being acquired by another company, or to calculate the fair value of stock market securities. However, fair value can be applied to almost any assessment of something's value.

WHY IT IS IMPORTANT

In the securities market, fair value explains the relationship between the futures contract on a market and the actual value of the index. In other words, if futures are trading above fair value, investors believe the index will rise. The opposite is true if futures are trading below fair value. If your business invests in futures, this can be crucial in your ability to raise finance. There will always be some variation around fair value because of short-term issues of supply and demand, but futures should generally be close to fair value.

HOW IT WORKS IN PRACTICE

The calculation of fair value is relatively simple as long as you have access to the necessary underlying data. The formula most often used is:

$$\text{Fair value} = \text{Cash} \times \frac{(1 + r \times x)}{360} - \text{Dividends}$$

where Cash is the closing index value, r is the current interest rate, and x is the time remaining until the contract expires, in days.

For example, the fair value calculation for the FTSE 100 where the closing price is 1157 points with a cash index of 1146, the interest rate is 0.57%, with 78 days before expiry of the contract, and a dividend value of 3.47 points, would be calculated as follows:

$$\text{Fair value} = 1146 \times \frac{(1 + 0.0057 \times 78)}{360} - 3.47$$

This calculation gives a fair value of 1156.68 points. If the FTSE is trading at 1157 then the difference between the two figures is 0.32. At this time, the stock is trading below fair value.

TRICKS OF THE TRADE

- Remember that fair value will change on a daily basis depending on the money markets.
- The key purpose of a fair value figure is to give investors a feel for the initial move of the markets "on the open." Futures trading above the fair value number indicate a positive open for the grouping discussed, while numbers below fair value are indicative of negative openings.
- Fair value can also be used to refer more generally to a stock trading at a reasonable level considering price/earning ratios.
- Many financial news websites publish fair value data daily for key global markets, which means that you may not need to do all the calculations manually.

MORE INFO

Website:

Mark Hanes on fair value: tinyurl.com/3lglrxf

Fixed-Deposit Compound Interest

WHAT IT MEASURES

The compound interest paid on fixed deposits, which is usually paid more frequently (monthly or quarterly) than a traditional annual interest rate. As the frequency of compounding increases, so does the effective rate of interest.

WHY IT IS IMPORTANT

The structure of fixed deposits means that a fixed-deposit investment offering a headline interest rate of, perhaps 8%, will in effect pay a rate higher than this. This must be taken into account, along with the frequency of compounding, when calculating the "effective" interest rate paid.

HOW IT WORKS IN PRACTICE

If your company invests $1 million at a rate of 8% for one year, at the end of the year the investment would be worth $1,080,000 based on annual compounding.

However, with fixed-deposit compound rates, interest may be paid more frequently, in which case the value of an investment changes. After one year, an investment of $1 million compounded quarterly would be worth £1,082,432 based on quarterly compounding, for example. This translates into an effective interest rate of 8.24%, rather than 8%.

The formula for calculating fixed deposit compound interest is as follows:

$$\text{FDCI} = p\left(1 + \frac{i}{m}\right)^{mt}$$

where:
p = investment
i = interest rate
m = number of times compounded per year
t = number of years

TRICKS OF THE TRADE

- With fixed-deposit investments, investors deposit a sum of money for a fixed period ranging from a few weeks to several years, which attracts a predetermined rate of interest. Fixed deposits are offered by banks and companies, although corporate fixed deposits are considered riskier.
- Fixed deposits offer regular income through interest payments, but won't offer the same returns as a stock portfolio—a typical fixed deposit compound interest rate is between 7% and 10%.

MORE INFO

Websites:

All Banking Solutions fixed deposit calculator: allbankingsolutions.com/fdcal.htm

MoneyChimp on compound interest: www.moneychimp.com/articles/finworks/fmfutval.htm

Yahoo compound interest calculator: tinyurl.com/6cko88p

See Also:

Annual Percentage Rate (pp. 24–25)
Nominal and Real Interest Rates (pp. 182–184)

Forward Interest Rates

WHAT THEY MEASURE

Forward interest rates are interest rates which are specified now for a loan or transaction that will occur at a specified future date. As with current interest rates, forward interest rates include a term structure which shows the different forward rates offered on transactions of different maturities. Forward rates are also known as implied forward rates.

WHY THEY ARE IMPORTANT

Forward interest rates are a vital part of forward rate agreements (FRAs), and are important in making any investment decision that is sensitive to interest rates. For corporations, this might include investments or loans, while investors will commonly use forward interest rates to compare forwards and futures for investment potential. Forward rates are also needed when you want to calculate the interest earned between two periods.

Forward rates are extrapolated from a risk-free theoretical spot rate, and should be monitored because they provide an insight into how the market is feeling about future movement of interest rates.

HOW THEY WORK IN PRACTICE

A conventional investment might offer an interest rate of 6.6% per annum, compounded annually. After two years, a $1 investment would return $1.14.

In a forward interest rate agreement, however, an investment and rate is agreed for a future date. For example, you might agree to invest $1 in one year's time, for a period of two years. The interest rate paid is a forward interest rate.

The payments on a forward interest rate agreement can be calculated using the following formula:

$$\text{Payment} = \text{Notional amount} \times \frac{(\text{Reference rate} - \text{Fixed rate} \times a)}{(1 + \text{Reference rate} \times a)}$$

where the reference rate is the base rate, usually taken from Libor, the fixed rate is the interest rate at which the loan is agreed, and α is the time/days involved, using dating conventions.

TRICKS OF THE TRADE

- Future interest rates can be calculated more accurately by incorporating discounted cash flow over the lifetime of the loan/investment. Given a discount function, it is possible to arrange today to borrow \$1 at the end of year 1 and pay 1/df(2) at the end of year 2 for a zero net investment, since each sum has a present value of \$1.
- Forward rates can cover periods that only last one period, with rates denoted by the starting date. For example, a year one forward rate covers the period from the end of year 1 to the end of year 2, but on terms negotiated today.
- Forward rates are also widely used in foreign currency exchange, where investors predict likely movements in rates over time. They can also be used to price bonds, using forward rates instead of discount rates to value the bond.

MORE INFO

Websites:

Forward rate agreement calculator: www.montegodata.co.uk/consult/FRA/fra.htm

Investopedia on forward rates: tinyurl.com/67pfnah

Future Value

Future value is simply the estimated value of a sum of money at a given point in the future, as in, "What will the $1,000 we have today be worth in two years' time?"

WHAT IT MEASURES

Any amount of any currency.

WHY IT IS IMPORTANT

Future value is a fundamental of investment. Understanding it helps any organization or individual to determine how a sum will be affected by changes in inflation, interest rates, or currency values. Inflation, for instance, will always reduce a sum's value. Interest rates will always increase it. Exchanging the sum for an identical amount in another currency will increase or decrease it, depending on how the respective currencies perform on the world market.

Armed with this knowledge, an organization can make more informed decisions about how to generate the maximum value from its funds in a given period of time: Would it be best to deposit them in simple interest-bearing accounts, exchange them for funds in another currency, use them to expand operations, or use them to acquire another company?

HOW IT WORKS IN PRACTICE

Start with three figures: the sum in question, the percentage by which it will increase or decrease, and the period of time. In this case: $1,000, 11%, and two years.

At an interest rate of 11%, our $1,000 will grow to $1,232 in two years:

$$\$1{,}000 \times 1.11 = \$1{,}110 \text{ (first year)} \times 1.11 = \$1{,}232 \text{ (second year)}$$

Note that the interest earned in the first year generates additional interest in the second year, a practice known as compounding.

When large sums are involved, the effect of compounding can be significant.

At an inflation rate of 11%, by contrast, our $1,000 will shrink to $812 in two years:

$$\frac{\$1{,}000}{1.11} = \frac{\$901 \text{ (first year)}}{1.11} = \$812 \text{ (second year)}$$

TRICKS OF THE TRADE

- Express the percentage as 1.11 and multiply and divide by that figure, instead of using 11%. Otherwise, errors will occur.
- Calculate each year, quarter, or month separately, as in our examples.
- It is important always to use the *annual* rates of interest and inflation.
- A more useful tool is "present value," which estimates what value future cash flows would have if they occurred today.

MORE INFO

Website:

Future value calculator: www.calculator.net/future-value-calculator.html

See Also:

Time Value of Money (pp. 255–257)

Future Value of an Annuity

Calculating the future value of an annuity is another example of the principle that money invested today will be worth more in the future.

WHAT IT MEASURES

The value to which a series of fixed-amount payments made at regular intervals will grow over the specified period of time.

WHY IT IS IMPORTANT

The calculation enables companies to determine the future value of a fund receiving regular payments, such as a pension fund to which contributions are made. Individuals in companies may find the calculation equally useful if they want to establish a fund to pay the cost of future college education: they will know what their annual payments will grow to be in a given number of years.

HOW IT WORKS IN PRACTICE

There are several types of annuity. They vary both in the ways they accumulate funds and in the ways they dispense earnings. The following are some examples:

- A **fixed annuity** guarantees fixed payments to the individual receiving it for the term of the contract, usually until death.
- A **variable annuity** offers no guarantee but has potential for a greater return, usually based on the performance of a stock or mutual fund.
- A **deferred annuity** delays payments until the individual chooses to receive them.
- A **hybrid annuity**, also called a combination annuity, combines features of both the fixed and variable annuity.

Financial calculators and spreadsheet programs will compute annuity calculations automatically. Manual calculations require a future-value-of-annuity table that contains figures based on the interest rate and period in question. The basic formula is:

Future value = Amount invested × Table value [interest, period]

If, for example, a pension manager puts $1,000,000 at the end of every year into his company's pension fund, the fund earns 8% interest, and there are no withdrawals, at the end of five years it will be worth:

$1,000,000 × 5.867 [table value] = $5,867,000

TRICKS OF THE TRADE

- The formula assumes that payments are made at the end of a given period.
- If a stated interest rate is not an annual rate, it must be adjusted to reflect an annual rate.
- Although their yields are low, annuities are relatively safe investments that provide level streams of cash flow for fixed periods of time.
- In the United States, annuities are tax-deferred, but also often carry an early withdrawal penalty.
- If you are calculating manually, be sure to use the designated future value of an annuity table, and not the future value table; there is a significant difference.
- The mathematical expression for the numbers appearing on a future value of an annuity table is $[(1 + i)^n - 1] \div i$; i is the interest rate, and n is the number of years in question.

MORE INFO

Book:

Walsh, Ciaran. *Key Management Ratios*. 4th ed. London: FT Prentice Hall, 2008.

Website:

Get Objects on future value of annuities: www.getobjects.com/Components/Finance/TVM/fva.html

Goodwill and Patents

One could define both goodwill and patents as figments of the imagination, the former a financier's and the latter an inventor's. The accounting realm assigns real value to both, based on the theory that both will deliver real benefits in the future.

WHAT IT MEASURES

The value of two intangible assets.

WHY IT IS IMPORTANT

Since both goodwill and patents are intangible assets, their values will be whatever negotiators conclude. Still, their values need to be reflected in financial statements. Goodwill is created in the aftermath of an acquisition, and must appear on a balance sheet. The acquisition of a patent has a cost of its own, be it the price of internal development costs, or the purchase price paid to an inventor.

HOW IT WORKS IN PRACTICE

Ultimately, the assigned values of both assets are matters of opinion, however learned the opinions may be. Each must be considered separately.

Ordinarily, goodwill is completely ignored by accountants. Only when a company has been acquired by another does goodwill become an intangible asset. It then appears on a balance sheet in the amount by which the price paid by the acquiring company exceeds the net tangible assets of the acquired company. In other words:

Goodwill = Purchase price − Net assets

If, for example, an airline is bought for $12 billion and its net assets are valued at $9 billion, $3 billion of the purchase would be allocated to goodwill on the balance sheet.

The buyer will attribute the difference to any number of reasons that give a competitive advantage, such as a loyal and long-standing customer base, a strong brand, strategic location, or productive employees.

A patent's value, meanwhile, will probably be the sum of its development costs, or its purchase price if acquired from someone else. It is usually to a company's advantage to spread the patent's value over several years. If so, the critical time period to consider is not the full life of the patent (17 years in the United States), but its estimated useful life.

For example, let's say that in January 2000 a company acquired a patent issued in January 1995 at a cost of $100,000. It concludes that the patent's useful commercial life is 10 years, not the 12 remaining before the patent expires. In turn, patent value would be $100,000, and it would be spread (or amortized in accounting terms) over 10 years, or $10,000 each year.

TRICKS OF THE TRADE

- Accounting for goodwill can vary by country, an issue that needs to be considered when evaluating or negotiating acquisitions of foreign-based companies. Moreover, the rules may change from time to time. In the United States, for example, goodwill no longer has to be amortized over 40 years.
- The total value of a patent's development costs may stretch over several years.
- The cost of a patent ultimately may have little bearing on the future revenues and profits it brings.

MORE INFO

Websites:

UK Intellectual Property Office on patents:
www.ipo.gov.uk/patent.htm

US Patent and Trademark Office on patents:
www.uspto.gov/patents/

Gross Profit Margin Ratio

WHAT IT MEASURES

The gross profit margin ratio measures how efficiently a company uses its resources, materials, and labor in the production process by showing the percentage of net sales remaining after subtracting the cost of making and selling a product or service. It is usually expressed as a percentage, and indicates the profitability of a business before overhead costs.

WHY IT IS IMPORTANT

A high gross profit margin ratio indicates that a business can make a reasonable profit on sales, as long as overheads do not increase. Investors pay attention to the gross profit margin ratio because it tells them how efficient your business is compared to competitors. It is sensible to track gross profit margin ratios over a number of years to see if company earnings are consistent, growing, or declining.

For businesses, knowing your gross profit margin ratio is important because it tells you whether your business is pricing goods and services effectively. A low margin compared to your competitors would suggest you are under-pricing, while a high margin might indicate over-pricing. Low profit margin ratios can also suggest the business is unable to control production costs, or that a low amount of earnings is generated from revenues.

HOW IT WORKS IN PRACTICE

To calculate gross profit margin ratio, use the following formula:

$$\text{Gross profit margin ratio} = \frac{\text{Gross profit margin}}{\text{Net sales}}$$

First, determine the gross profit for the business during a specific period of time, such as a financial quarter. This is total revenue minus the cost of sales. The cost of sales includes variable costs associated with manufacturing, packaging, and freight, and should not include fixed overheads such as rent or utilities.

For example, if Company A has net sales of $10 million, while costs for inventory or production total $7 million, then the gross profit margin is $3 million. Next, divide this by net sales. In our example:

$$\frac{3{,}000{,}000}{10{,}000{,}000} = 0.3 = 30\%$$

(Simply multiply the result by 100 to see it expressed as a percentage, here a gross profit margin ratio of 30%.) Tracking several subsequent quarters will allow you to create a more accurate profit margin ratio. A more detailed version of the formula is:

$$\text{Gross profit margin ratio} = \frac{(\text{Total revenue} - \text{Cost of sales})}{\text{Total sales}}$$

TRICKS OF THE TRADE

- Gross profit margins tend to remain stable over time. Significant irregularities or sudden variations might be a potential sign of financial fraud, accounting irregularities, or problems in the business.
- Gross profit margin ratios can be calculated alongside net profit margin ratios (net profit after tax ÷ sales), pre-tax profit margins (net profit before tax ÷ sales), and operating profit margins (net income before interest and taxes ÷ sales) to provide a more comprehensive insight into margins. Net profit margins and gross profit margins can be significantly different because of the impact of interest and tax expenses.
- Profit margin ratios are a popular way to benchmark against competitors. Industries will generally have standard gross profit margin ratios, which are easily discovered.
- If you use an accounting program such as QuickBooks, the software can calculate gross profit margin ratios for you, making it easier to track margin ratios over several years. If you discover

fluctuations regularly occur at a particular time of year, you might try to adjust pricing to encourage greater sales at that period.

MORE INFO

Websites:

About.com on gross profit margin: tinyurl.com/e5b3b

BizWiz Consulting on profit margin ratios: tinyurl.com/6aykdyk

Interest Coverage

Interest coverage, or interest cover, describes several ratios used to assess a company's financial strength and capital structure.

WHAT IT MEASURES

The amount of earnings available to make interest payments after all operating and nonoperating income and expenses—except interest and income taxes—have been accounted for.

WHY IT IS IMPORTANT

Interest coverage is regarded as a measure of a company's creditworthiness because it shows how much income there is to cover interest payments on outstanding debt. Banks and financial analysts also rely on this ratio as a rule of thumb to gauge the fundamental strength of a business.

HOW IT WORKS IN PRACTICE

Interest coverage is expressed as a ratio, and reflects a company's ability to pay the interest obligations on its debt. It compares the funds available to pay interest—earnings before interest and taxes, or EBIT—with the interest expense. The basic formula is:

$$\text{Interest coverage ratio} = \frac{\text{EBIT}}{\text{Interest expense}}$$

If interest expense for a year is $9 million, and the company's EBIT is $45 million, the interest coverage would be:

$$\frac{45{,}000{,}000}{9{,}000{,}000} = 5$$

The higher the number, the stronger a company is likely to be. Conversely, a low number suggests that a company's fortunes are looking ominous. Variations of this basic formula also exist. For example, there is:

$$\text{Cash flow interest coverage ratio} = \frac{(\text{Operating cash flow} + \text{Interest} + \text{Taxes})}{\text{Interest}}$$

This ratio indicates the company's ability to use its cash flow to satisfy its fixed financing obligations. Finally, there is the fixed-charge coverage ratio, which compares EBIT with fixed charges:

$$\text{Fixed-charge coverage ratio} = \frac{(\text{EBIT} + \text{Lease expenses})}{(\text{Interest} + \text{Lease expense})}$$

"Fixed charges" can be interpreted in many ways, however. It could mean, for example, the funds that a company is obliged to set aside to retire debt, or dividends on preferred stock.

TRICKS OF THE TRADE

- A ratio of less than 1 indicates that a company is having problems generating enough cash flow to pay its interest expenses, and that either a modest decline in operating profits or a sudden rise in borrowing costs could eliminate profitability entirely.
- Ideally, interest coverage should at least exceed 1.5; in some sectors, 2.0 or higher is desirable.
- Interest coverage is widely considered to be more meaningful than looking at total debt, because what really matters is what an enterprise must pay in a given period, not how much debt it has.
- As is often the case, it may be more meaningful to watch interest coverage over several periods in order to detect long-term trends.
- Cash flow will sometimes be substituted for EBIT in the ratio, because EBIT includes not only cash but also accrued sales and other unrealized income.
- Interest coverage also is called "times interest earned."

Internal Rate of Return

Internal rate of return (IRR) is another analytical tool based on the time value of money principle. Some regard it as the companion to net present value.

WHAT IT MEASURES

Technically, the interest rate that makes the present value of an investment's projected cash flows equal to the cost of the project; practically speaking, the rate that indicates whether or not an investment is worth pursuing.

WHY IT IS IMPORTANT

The calculation of internal rate of return (IRR) is used to appraise the prospective viability of investments and capital projects. It is also called dollar-weighted rate of return.

Essentially, IRR allows an investor to find the interest rate that is equivalent to the monetary returns expected from the project. Once that rate is determined, it can be compared to the rates that could be earned by investing the money elsewhere, or to the weighted cost of capital. IRR also accounts for the time value of money.

HOW IT WORKS IN PRACTICE

How is IRR applied? Assume, for example, that a project under consideration costs $7,500 and is expected to return $2,000 per year for five years, or $10,000. The IRR calculated for the project would be about 10%. If the cost of borrowing money for the project, or the return on investing the funds elsewhere, is less than 10%, the project is probably worthwhile. If the alternate use of the money will return 10% or more, the project should be rejected, since from a financial perspective it will break even at best.

Typically, management requires an IRR equal to or higher than the cost of capital, depending on relative risk and other factors.

The best way to compute an IRR is by using a spreadsheet (such as Excel) or a financial calculator, which do it automatically, although it is crucial to understand how the calculation should be structured. Calculating IRR by hand is tedious and time-consuming, and requires the process to be repeated to run sensitivities.

If using Excel, for example, select the IRR function. This requires the annual cash flows to be set out in columns, and the first part of the IRR formula requires the cell reference range of these cash flows to be entered. Then a guess of the IRR is required. The default is 10%, written 0.1.

If a project has the following expected cash flows, then guessing IRR at 30% returns an accurate IRR of 27%, indicating that if the next best way of investing the money gives a return of –20%, the project should go ahead.

Now	-2,500
Year 1	1,200
Year 2	1,300
Year 3	1,500

TRICKS OF THE TRADE

- IRR analysis is generally used to evaluate a project's cash flows rather than income because, unlike income, cash flows do not reflect depreciation and therefore are usually more instructive to appraise.
- Most basic spreadsheet functions apply to cash flows only.
- As well as advocates, IRR has critics who dismiss it as misleading, especially as significant costs will occur late in the project. The rule of thumb that "the higher the IRR the better" does not always apply.
- For the most thorough analysis of a project's investment potential, some experts urge using both IRR and net present value calculations, and comparing their results.

MORE INFO

Book:

Walsh, Ciaran. *Key Management Ratios*. 4th ed. London: FT Prentice Hall, 2008.

Article:

Baker, Samuel L. "The internal rate of return." March 28, 2006. Online at: sambaker.com/econ/irr/irr.html

Liquidity Ratio Analysis

WHAT IT MEASURES

Liquidity ratios are a set of ratios or figures that measure a company's ability to pay off its short-term debt obligations. This is done by measuring a company's liquid assets (including those that might easily be converted into cash) against its short-term liabilities.

There are a number of different liquidity ratios, which each measure slightly different types of assets when calculating the ratio. More conservative measures will exclude assets that need to be converted into cash.

WHY IT IS IMPORTANT

In general, the greater the coverage of liquid assets to short-term liabilities, the more likely it is that a business will be able to pay debts as they become due while still funding ongoing operations. On the other hand, a company with a low liquidity ratio might have difficulty meeting obligations while funding vital ongoing business operations.

Liquidity ratios are sometimes requested by banks when they are evaluating a loan application. If you take out a loan, the lender may require you to maintain a certain minimum liquidity ratio, as part of the loan agreement. For that reason, steps to improve your liquidity ratios are sometimes necessary.

HOW IT WORKS IN PRACTICE

There are three fundamental liquidity ratios that can provide insight into short-term liquidity: current, quick, and cash ratios. These work as follows:

Current Ratio

This is a way of testing liquidity by deriving the proportion of assets available to cover current liabilities, as follows:

$$\text{Current ratio} = \frac{\text{Current assets}}{\text{Current liabilities}}$$

Current ratio is widely discussed in the financial world, and it is easy to understand. However, it can be misleading because the chances of a company ever needing to liquidate all its assets to meet liabilities are very slim indeed. It is often more useful to consider a company as a going concern, in which case you need to understand the time it takes to convert assets into cash, as well as the current ratio.

The current ratio should be at least between 1.5 and 2, although some investors would argue that the figure should be above 2, particularly if a high proportion of assets are stock. A ratio of less than 1 (that is, where the current liabilities exceed the current assets) could mean that you are unable to meet debts as they fall due, in which case you are insolvent. A high current ratio could indicate that too much money is tied up in current assets—for example, giving customers too much credit.

Cash Ratio

This indicates liquidity by measuring the amount of cash, cash equivalents, and invested funds that are available to meet current short-term liabilities. It is calculated by using the following formula:

$$\text{Cash ratio} = \frac{(\text{Cash} + \text{Cash equivalents} + \text{Invested funds})}{\text{Current liabilities}}$$

The cash ratio is a more conservative measure of liquidity than the current ratio, because it only looks at assets that are already liquid, ignoring assets such as receivables or inventory.

Quick Ratio

The third liquidity ratio is a more sophisticated alternative to the current ratio, which measures the most liquid current assets—excluding inventory but including accounts receivable and certain investments.

$$\text{Quick ratio} = \frac{(\text{Cash equivalents} + \text{Short-term investments} + \text{Accounts receivable})}{\text{Current liabilities}}$$

The quick ratio should be around 0.7–1, with very few companies having a cash ratio of over 1. To be absolutely safe, the quick ratio should be at least 1, which indicates that quick assets exceed current liabilities. If the current ratio is rising and the quick ratio is static, this suggests a potential stockholding problem.

TRICKS OF THE TRADE

- All of these ratios have advantages and disadvantages. It is important to remember that any ratio that includes accounts receivable assumes a liquidation of accounts receivable—this may not be possible, practical, or desirable in many situations.
- Liquidity ratios should therefore be considered alongside ratios demonstrating the time it would take to convert assets to cash—a conversion time of several months compared to a few days would seriously affect liquidity.
- Some analysts use a fourth liquidity ratio to measure business performance, known as the "defensive interval." This measures how long a business can survive without cash coming in—and ideally should be between 30 and 90 days.

MORE INFO

Book:

Berman, Karen, and Joe Knight, with John Case. "Liquidity ratios: Can we pay our bills?" In *Financial Intelligence: A Manager's Guide to Knowing What the Numbers Really Mean*. Boston, MA: Harvard Business School Press, 2005. Also available separately.

See Also:

Acid-Test Ratio (pp. 7–9)
Current Ratio (pp. 93–94)

Management Accounts

WHAT THEY MEASURE

Company accounts fall into two categories: financial and management. While financial accounts are regulated and audited reports of financial transactions and processes, the management accounts are designed to help key business executives understand the overall performance of the business. Most companies produce these reports monthly or quarterly.

WHY THEY ARE IMPORTANT

Rather than focusing on financial metrics, management accounting focuses on operations and the value chain, as opposed to the historical activities of external financial reporting and auditing. They tend to be forward-looking and focused on identifying new revenue, cash flow, profit forecasts, and growth opportunities. Management accounts help executives carry out planning, control, and administration duties effectively. They mean you can see whether profitable parts of the business are subsidizing less successful activities, you can compare performance with forecasts, can identify trends, and manage resources better.

HOW THEY WORK IN PRACTICE

At their most basic, management accounts are reports that provide analysis of business performance and strategy broken down into different business activities or products. Each section of the report should provide an overview of cash flow, profit margins, liabilities, and forecasts for key business metrics.

In practice, management accounts are usually more complex than this. Management accountants may follow any of a number of management accounting methodologies, which will dictate what information is collected, and how it might be presented. Popular approaches to management accounting include:

Lifecycle costing: A form of management accounting that analyses the cost of manufacturing an individual product or service, and looks for how this might be improved.

Activity-based costing: Considers the costs involved in key manufacturing and business processes, such as running a single payroll, or a single product manufacturing cycle.

GPK: A German methodology for management accounting, sometimes known as marginal planned cost accounting. This system was created to provide a consistent, accurate view of how managerial costs are calculated and assigned to a company's products and services.

Lean accounting: A management accounting methodology that was designed in the 1990s for use in just-in-time manufacturing environments and service businesses.

Resource consumption accounting: Focuses on identifying areas with potential for business optimization. Governed by the RCA Institute, this approach to accounting promotes consistency and professionalism in management accounts.

Throughput accounting: Recognizes the relationships between the various elements of the modern manufacturing process, and uses calculations to measure the contribution each part makes per unit of resource.

Management accounting can be applied to virtually any business, and each methodology can be tailored to meet the needs of different industries and sizes of company. However, any management accounting program should incorporate most of the following elements:

- variance analysis;
- rate and volume analysis;
- price modeling and profit margin analysis;
- cost analysis;
- cost/benefit analysis;
- lifecycle cost analysis;
- capital budgeting;
- strategic analysis;
- annual budgeting;
- sales and financial forecasting;
- cost allocation.

TRICKS OF THE TRADE

- Management accounting is easier if you build in regular systems to capture key information on a daily or weekly basis. Day to day, business managers should record information into a management accounts spreadsheet or application, including details of transactions made, results of financial changes, and projections of future trade.
- There are many off-the-shelf software packages that can be used for this purpose. The key is to select something easy to use—it's not an effective use of resources to spend weeks learning the intricacies of a financial reporting tool if your job is not financial.
- There is no pre-determined format for management accounts, nor any legal requirement to prepare them—but few businesses can survive without them.

MORE INFO

Website:

Arts Council England management accounts templates: tinyurl.com/ovf7egl

Marginal Cost

Marginal cost is based on the economic theory that the more goods are produced, the lower will be the per-unit cost.

WHAT IT MEASURES

The additional cost of producing one more unit of product, or providing service to one more customer.

WHY IT IS IMPORTANT

Sometimes called incremental cost, marginal cost shows how much costs increase from making or serving one more unit, an essential factor when contemplating a production increase, or seeking to serve more customers.

If the price charged is greater than the marginal cost, then the revenue gain will be greater than the added cost. That, in turn, will increase profit, so the expansion in production or service makes economic sense and should proceed. Of course, the reverse is also true: If the price charged is less than the marginal cost, expansion should not go ahead.

HOW IT WORKS IN PRACTICE

The formula for marginal cost is:

$$\text{Marginal cost} = \frac{\text{Change in cost}}{\text{Change in quantity}}$$

If it costs a company $260,000 to produce 3,000 items, and $325,000 to produce 3,800 items, the change in cost would be:

325,000 − 260,000 = $65,000

The change in quantity would be:

3,800 − 3,000 = 800

When the formula to calculate marginal cost is applied, the result is:

$$\frac{65{,}000}{800} = \$81.25$$

If the price of the item in question were, say, $99.95, expansion should proceed.

TRICKS OF THE TRADE

- A marginal cost that is lower than the price shows that it is not always necessary to cut prices to sell more goods and boost profits.
- Using idle capacity to produce lower-margin items can still be beneficial, because these generate revenues that help cover fixed costs.
- Marginal cost studies can become quite complicated, because the basic formula does not always take into account variables that can affect cost and quantity. Software programs are available, many of which are industry-specific.
- At some point, marginal cost invariably begins to rise; typically, labor becomes less productive as a production run increases, while the time required also increases.
- Marginal cost alone may not justify expansion. It is best to determine also average costs, then chart the respective series of figures to find where marginal cost meets average cost, and thus determine optimum cost.
- Relying on marginal cost is not fail-safe; putting more product on a market can drive down prices and thus cut margins. Moreover, committing idle capacity to long-term production may tie up resources that could be directed to a new and more profitable opportunity.
- An important related principle is contribution: the cash gained (or lost) from selling an additional unit.

Marginal Rate of Substitution

WHAT IT MEASURES

Sometimes referred to as MRS, the marginal rate of substitution measures the rate at which an individual must give up one asset to obtain a single additional unit of a second asset, while keeping overall utility constant. MRS can measure physical goods, but also assets such as labor or time. The result is generally plotted on an "indifference curve," which shows the utility value for each combination of assets. MRS is also often used to show the rate at which a consumer will substitute one product or service with an alternative.

WHY IT IS IMPORTANT

MRS enables businesses to analyze how a rational user/consumer/-organization chooses between two goods. For example, how will a change in the wage rate affect the choice between leisure time and work time? How far will price increases affect a consumer's choice of drinking water?

HOW IT WORKS IN PRACTICE

To calculate MRS, we begin by creating an indifference curve, a line showing all the possible combinations of two goods/assets. The line plots the combinations that result in the same utility or value to the consumer.

In Figure 1, the graph shows a person receives the same utility from 4 hours of work and 6 hours of leisure as from 7 hours of work and 3 hours of leisure.

MRS is the amount of one asset (leisure) that needs to be sacrificed to obtain one unit of the second asset (work) while achieving the same utility (satisfaction).

The simple equation to calculate MRS is as follows:

$$\text{Marginal rate of substitution} = \frac{-dy}{dx}$$

where d = change in good, and x and y represent different goods, products, or services. This calculation assumes utility remains constant.

Figure 1. An example indifference curve

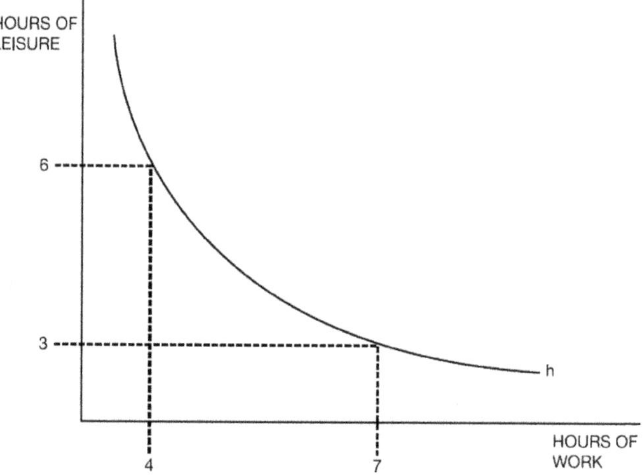

For example, if the MRS is 2 then the consumer will give up 2 units of y to obtain one additional unit of x.

Using the example above, the marginal rate of substitution between the two selected variables is:

$$\frac{-(6-3)}{(4-7)} = \frac{-3}{-3} = 1$$

TRICKS OF THE TRADE

- Marginal rate of substitution diminishes over time because there is a principle of diminishing marginal utility—so the more units are consumed, the less additional satisfaction each addition

creates (in other words, the more we consume something, the more willing we are to substitute it away).
- It is possible to create graphs showing more than one indifference curve—in this case, the resulting graph is called an "indifference curve map."
- A key limitation of MRS is that the relationship between two goods remains constant. In reality, it may be that as a worker increases their salary, they desire more leisure time because they have more disposable income. An increase in tea consumption may decrease the marginal utility of coffee.
- It is common to add a budget line to MRS graphs, to separate affordable and unaffordable consumption possibilities.

MORE INFO

Book:

Pindyck, Robert S., and Daniel L. Rubinfeld. *Microeconomics*. 7th ed. Upper Saddle River, NJ: Pearson/Prentice Hall, 2008.

Website:

Answers.com on MRS:
www.answers.com/topic/marginal-rate-of-substitution

Market/Book Ratio

WHAT IT MEASURES

Market/book ratio, sometimes called price-to-book ratio, is a way of measuring the relative value of a company compared to its stock price or market value.

WHY IT IS IMPORTANT

Market/book ratio is a useful way of measuring your company's performance and making quick comparisons with competitors. It is an essential figure to potential investors and analysts because it provides a simple way of judging whether a company is under or overvalued. If your business has a low market/book ratio, it's considered a good investment opportunity.

HOW IT WORKS IN PRACTICE

At its simplest, market/book ratio measures the market capitalization (expressed as price per stock) of a business divided by its book value (the value of assets minus liabilities). The book value of a company refers to what would be left if the business paid its liabilities and shut its doors, although, of course, a growing business will always be worth more than its book value because it has the ability to generate new sales.

To calculate market/book ratio, take the current price per stock and divide by the book value per stock:

$$\text{Market/book ratio} = \frac{\text{Market price per stock}}{\text{Book value per stock}}$$

For example, Company A might be trading at $2.20 per stock. However, the book value per stock is actually $3.00. This results in a market/book ratio of 0.73, suggesting the company's assets may in fact be undervalued by 27%.

Market-to-book value can alternatively be calculated as follows:

$$\text{Market/book ratio} = \frac{\text{Market price per stock}}{\text{Net asset value per stock}}$$

TRICKS OF THE TRADE

- Like the price-to-earnings ratio, the lower the price-to-book ratio or market/book ratio, the better the value. Investors would use a low price-to-book ratio on stock screens, for instance, to identify potential candidates for new investment. As a rule of thumb, a market/book ratio above one suggests the company is undervalued, while a ratio over one suggests the company might be overvalued.
- A low market/book ratio could suggest a company's assets are undervalued, or that the company's prospects are good and earnings/value should grow.
- Market/book ratios are most useful when valuing knowledge-intensive companies, where physical assets may not accurately or fully reflect the value of the business. Technology companies and other businesses that don't have a lot of physical assets tend to have low book-to-market ratios.

MORE INFO

See Also:

Book Value (pp. 41–42)

Net Added Value (NAV) and Adjusted NAV

WHAT IT MEASURES

Net added value, or net asset value, is the value of a corporate asset or business based on its assets minus its liabilities. Adjusted NAV refers to the value once it has been adjusted for any known or suspected differences between market value and book value. In share dealing, NAV refers to the value of a portfolio minus its liabilities.

WHY IT IS IMPORTANT

For investors, the NAV gives an idea of appropriate share prices. For example, if a fund's NAV is $10, you should expect that you can buy the fund's shares for $10 each, although there are exceptions to this rule, such as a newly launched fund. NAV is particularly important when valuing shares in companies where much of the value comes from assets rather than the profit stream—such as investment trusts, but also property companies.

HOW IT WORKS IN PRACTICE

To calculate NAV for an investment portfolio, you should use the following formula:

$$\text{Net added value} = \frac{(\text{Market value of all securities} + \text{Cash} + \text{Equivalent holdings} - \text{Liabilities})}{\text{Total shares outstanding}}$$

For example, if a mutual fund holds $10.5 million in securities, $2 million in cash, and has liabilities totaling $0.5 million, with one million shares outstanding, then the NAV calculation would be as follows:

$$\frac{(10.5 + 2 - 0.5)}{1} = \$12$$

TRICKS OF THE TRADE

- When calculating NAV for collective investments such as mutual funds, NAV is the total value of the portfolio less liabilities, calculated on a daily basis. Another alternative measurement for NAV is to add together unit capital and reserves held by a fund.
- In corporate valuations, NAV is the value of assets less liabilities. Assets include anything owned, whether in possession or not, while a liability is anything that is a potential cost to the business. Obviously this means calculating NAV for corporate entities is more difficult, and might be based on book value, carrying value, historical costs, amortized cost, or market value.
- NAV is a good way to keep track of price changes and asset valuations. However, you should keep in mind that the NAV calculation will change from day to day, and does not necessarily reflect the performance of the fund. In the early days of a fund, NAV will rise and fall as the fund's managers take their fees, and each time the fund makes a payout to shareholders. When a fund opens, it often trades at a premium to NAV, later falling to a discount.
- In general, a low NAV is considered a better investment opportunity than a high NAV. However, because NAV values on investment portfolios are calculated daily, critics argue that they are not a good performance indicator.
- In mutual funds, NAV per share is calculated at the close of trading each day based on closing share prices of securities held in the fund's portfolio. Any buy and sell orders are processed based on the day's NAV.
- The price that investors pay to purchase unit trust units is based on the approximate NAV per unit, plus fees that will be imposed by the unit's managers such as purchase fees.
- While you can calculate NAV for almost any business or fund, it is not of any real use when applied to service companies where there are few assets of value, such as plants, property, or equipment.

MORE INFO

Websites:

Money Terms on NAV: moneyterms.co.uk/nav/

US SEC on NAV: www.sec.gov/answers/nav.htm

Net Present Value

Net present value (NPV) expresses the sum total of an investment's future net cash flows (receipts less payments) minus the investment's initial costs. It is an investment appraisal tool.

WHAT IT MEASURES

The projected profitability of an investment, based on anticipated cash flows and discounted at a stated rate of interest.

WHY IT IS IMPORTANT

Net present value helps management or potential investors weigh the wisdom of an investment—in new equipment, a new facility, or other type of asset—by enabling them to quantify the expected benefits. Those evaluating more than one potential investment can compare the respective projected returns to find the most attractive project.

A positive NPV indicates that the project should be profitable, assuming that the estimated cash flows are reasonably accurate. A negative NPV, of course, indicates that the project will probably be unprofitable and therefore should be adjusted, if not abandoned altogether.

Equally significantly, NPV enables a management to consider the time value of money it will invest. This concept holds that the value of money increases with time because it can always earn interest in a savings account. Therefore, any other investment of that money must be weighed against how the funds would perform if simply deposited and saved.

When the time value of money concept is incorporated in the calculation of NPV, the value of a project's future net cash receipts in "today's money" can be determined. This enables proper comparisons between different projects.

HOW IT WORKS IN PRACTICE

Let's say that Global Manufacturing Inc. is considering the acquisition of a new machine. First, its management would consider all the factors: Initial purchase and installation costs; additional revenues generated by sales of the new machine's products; and the taxes on these new revenues. Having accounted for these factors in its calculations, the cash flows that Global Manufacturing projects will generate from the new machine are:

Year 1	–$100,000 (initial cost of investment)
Year 2	$30,000
Year 3	$40,000
Year 4	$40,000
Year 5	$35,000
Net total	$145,000

At first glance, it appears that cash flows total a whopping 45% more than the $100,000 initial cost, a strikingly sound investment indeed.

Alas, it's not that simple. Time value of money shrinks return on the project considerably, since future dollars are worth less than present dollars in hand. NPV accounts for these differences with the help of present value tables. These user-friendly tables, readily available on the internet and in references, list the ratios that express the present value of expected cash flow dollars, based on the applicable interest rate and the number of years in question.

In our example, Global Manufacturing's cost of capital is 9%. Using this figure to find the corresponding ratios in the present value table, the $100,000 investment cost, and expected annual revenues during the five years in question, the NPV calculation looks like this:

Year	Cash flow	Table factor (at 9%)	Present value
1	– $100,000	× 1.000000	= – $100,000.00
2	$30,000	× 0.917431	= $27,522.93
3	$40,000	× 0.841680	= $33,667.20
4	$40,000	× 0.772183	= $30,887.32
5	$35,000	× 0.708425	= $24,794.88
NPV			$16,873.33

Summing the present values of the cash flows and subtracting the investment cost from the total, the NPV is still positive. So, on this basis at least, the investment should proceed.

TRICKS OF THE TRADE

- Beware of assumptions. Interest rates change, of course, which can affect NPV dramatically. Moreover, fresh revenues (as well as new markets) may not grow as projected. If the cash flows in years 2–5 of our example fall by $5,000 a year, for instance, NPV shrinks to $5,260.89, which is still positive but less attractive.
- NPV calculations are performed only with cash receipts payments and discounting factors. In turn, NPV is a tool, not *the* tool. It ignores other accounting data, intangibles, sheer faith in a new idea, and other factors that may make an investment worth pursuing despite a negative NPV.
- It is important to determine a company's cost of capital accurately.

MORE INFO

Book:

Walsh, Ciaran. *Key Management Ratios*. 4th ed. London: FT Prentice Hall, 2008.

Nominal and Real Interest Rates

WHAT THEY MEASURE

When calculating interest rates, the nominal rate of interest refers to an interest rate calculated without any adjustment for inflation or for the full effect of compounding. The real interest rate includes compensation for value lost through inflation, whereas the nominal rate excludes this. Finally, the effective interest rate (sometimes known as the annual equivalent rate, or AER) is a rate that takes account of the impact of compounding.

If you purchase a bond for one year that pays 6% interest at the end of the 12 months, a $100 investment would return $106. The 6% interest is a nominal interest rate—it does not account for inflation during that year.

Imagine investing in the same bond and accounting for a 3% inflation rate for the year. If you buy an item for $100 at the start of the year, the same item would cost $103 at the end of the year. If we then invest the $100 into the 6% bond for one year, we lose $3 to inflation—meaning the real interest rate of the bond is actually 3%.

Alternatively, imagine investing the same $100 into the bond over 12 months. At 6%, your money would return $106 after one year. However, if interest is compounded every six months, you will actually earn slightly more. After six months, you would earn $3 interest. At the end of the year, the bond will pay 3% of your new investment total of $103, or $3.09. Your investment would then return $106.09 over a year, making the effective annual rate 6.09%, slightly higher than the nominal interest rate of 6%.

WHY THEY ARE IMPORTANT

When calculating interest rates, most calculations ignore the cost to the lender of not having funds available for a period of time—by the time a loan is repaid, the cost of items may have increased so that the money is now worth less. If you know what inflation is going to be, real interest rates are a powerful tool in analyzing the value of potential investments, because they take account of the erosion of spending power over the lifetime of an investment.

Calculating the effective rate is important because interest on different investments might be paid weekly, monthly, or annually. The effective annual interest rate can compare the returns or costs of different loans more accurately than a nominal interest rate.

HOW THEY WORK IN PRACTICE

The difference between real and nominal interest rates is simply expressed as: Real interest rate = Nominal rate − Inflation. More formally, it can also be described in the equation:

$$(1 + N) = (1 + r) - (1 + i)$$

where:
N is the nominal interest rate;
r is the real interest rate;
i is the rate of inflation.

This calculation is sometimes referred to as the Fisher equation. If you do not know the rate of inflation, it can be predicted using the following formula:

$$i = \frac{(\text{CPI this year} - \text{CPI last year})}{\text{CPI last year}}$$

If you know the nominal interest rate and the number of compounding periods, it is possible to calculate the effective annual rate using the following formula:

$$\text{EAR} = (1 + N/P)^{P-1}$$

where:
N is the nominal rate;
P is the number of compounding periods.

TRICKS OF THE TRADE

- If inflation is positive then the real interest rate will be lower than the nominal interest rate. If the economy is experiencing deflation and the inflation rate is negative, then real interest is higher than nominal interest rates.

- When calculating effective interest rates, remember they will generally not include one-off charges such as set-up fees. In addition, while financial regulators closely control how the APR is expressed, there are fewer controls on the AER.
- The Fisher hypothesis states that, over time, inflation and nominal interest rates move together, so real interest rates are stable in the long term. This theory—sometimes called the Fisher effect, was devised by Irving Fisher.
- Some bonds and savings products link payments to an inflation index, so in effect pay a real interest rate. An example would be government-issued gilt.
- Sometimes it can be beneficial to value investments without taking inflation into account. This can be done by discounting using real interest rates.

MORE INFO

Article:

Moffatt, Mike. "What's the difference between nominal and real? Real variables and nominal variables explained." *About.com*. Online at: tinyurl.com/q25tt

See Also:

Annual Percentage Rate (pp. 24–25)
Fixed-Deposit Compound Interest (pp. 145–146)

Option Pricing

WHAT IT MEASURES

There are two sorts of options in stock market trading: call and put. Option pricing uses mathematical models to calculate the value of a stock option and how it changes in response to changing conditions.

There are two key components to option pricing: the intrinsic value, which measures the amount by which an option is "in the money;" and the time value, which measures the amount paid for the time the option has before it expires.

WHY IT IS IMPORTANT

Stock traders use option pricing models to predict which options can be used to capture a potential move in a stock, and gain advantage in a trade. Option pricing is also important in risk management, because it can be used to quantify the risk associated with buying, selling, owning, and trading specific options with a high level of accuracy.

HOW IT WORKS IN PRACTICE

To understand option pricing, you must understand the four basic drivers of option prices: current stock price, intrinsic value, time to expiration, and volatility.

Stock price is important because if the price of a stock rises, the cost of a call option will also rise (though not necessarily at the same rate).

Intrinsic value is important because it measures how far an option is "in the money" (ITM), or what proportion of the option's value isn't lost over time. The intrinsic value of the call option is the stock price minus the call strike price.

Time value is the difference between the option's price and its intrinsic value. The more time an option has until it expires, the greater chance it will become "in the money"—and therefore the option becomes more valuable.

Option pricing is related to volatility expected in the market up to the time of expiration. If the market expects little movement in a stock's value, volatility is low, which results in a lower time value.

The most well-known method of modeling option pricing was developed by Fischer Black and Myron Scholes in 1973. The Black–Scholes model works as follows:

$$C = SN(d_1) - Ke^{(-rt)} N(d_2)$$

where:
C = call premium;
S = current stock price;
t = time to expiration;
K = option price;
r = risk-free interest rate;
N = normal distribution;
e = exponential term.

The first part of the calculation, $SN(d_1)$, shows the expected benefit of buying the stock outright. This is calculated by multiplying together the stock price and the change in call premium caused by a change in the underlying stock price.

The second part of the equation shows the present value of paying the exit price on the day the option expires. The fair value of the option price is then calculated by looking at the difference between the option's current value and value at expiration.

The Black–Scholes model of option pricing relies on several assumptions, which should be taken into account. These are:

- the stock pays no dividends during the option's life;
- the stock can only be exercised on the expiration date;
- markets are efficient;
- no commissions are charged;
- interest rates are consistent, predictable, and known;
- returns are normally distributed.

TRICKS OF THE TRADE

- A major potential limitation of the Black–Scholes model is the assumption that no dividends are paid on stock during the lifetime of the option—because most stocks do pay dividends. One way to resolve this is to subtract the discounted value of a future dividend from the stock price.
- In Europe, it is common that options can only be exercised on the expiration date, whereas in the United States they might be exercised at any time. This makes American options more flexible and therefore more valuable.
- The Black–Scholes model has been refined over time by a number of financial scholars, including Merton (who devised a model to take account of dividends) and Ingerson (who devised a model that did not require constant interest rates).

MORE INFO

Article:

Wagner, Hans. "Understanding option pricing." *Investopedia* (April 20, 2009). Online at: tinyurl.com/6l3n837

Website:

Risk Glossary on option pricing theory: tinyurl.com/6gq7u3f

Payback Period

At first glance, payback is a simple investment appraisal technique, but it can quickly become complex.

WHAT IT MEASURES

How long it will take to earn back the money invested in a project.

WHY IT IS IMPORTANT

The straight payback period method is the simplest way of determining the investment potential of a major project. Expressed in time, it tells a management how many months or years it will take to recover the original cash cost of the project—always a vital consideration, and especially so for managements evaluating several projects at once.

This evaluation becomes even more important if it includes an examination of what the present value of future revenues will be.

HOW IT WORKS IN PRACTICE

The straight payback period formula is:

$$\text{Payback period} = \frac{\text{Cost of project}}{\text{Annual cash revenues}}$$

Thus, if a project costs \$100,000 and is expected to generate \$28,000 annually, the payback period would be:

$$\frac{100{,}000}{28{,}000} = 3.57 \text{ years}$$

If the revenues generated by the project are expected to vary from year to year, add the revenues expected for each succeeding year until you arrive at the total cost of the project.

For example, say the revenues expected to be generated by the \$100,000 project are:

Year	Revenue	Total
1	$19,000	$19,000
2	$25,000	$44,000
3	$30,000	$74,000
4	$30,000	$104,000
5	$30,000	$134,000

Thus, the project would be fully paid for in year 4, since it is in that year that the total revenue reaches the initial cost of $100,000.

The picture becomes complex when the time value of money principle is introduced into the calculations. Some experts insist this is essential to determine the most accurate payback period. Accordingly, present value tables or computers (now the norm) must be used, and the annual revenues have to be discounted by the applicable interest rate, 10% in this example. Doing so produces significantly different results:

Year	Revenue	Present value	Total
1	$19,000	$17,271	$17,271
2	$25,000	$20,650	$37,921
3	$30,000	$22,530	$60,451
4	$30,000	$20,490	$80,941
5	$30,000	$18,630	$99,571

This method shows that payback would not occur even after five years.

TRICKS OF THE TRADE

- Clearly, a main defect of the straight payback period method is that it ignores the time value of money principle, which, in turn, can produce unrealistic expectations.
- A second drawback is that it ignores any benefits generated after the payback period, and thus a project that would return $1 million after, say, six years might be ranked lower than a project with a three-year payback that returns only $100,000 thereafter.

- Another alternative to calculating by payback period is to develop an internal rate of return.
- Under most analyses, projects with shorter payback periods rank higher than those with longer paybacks, even if the latter promise higher returns. Longer paybacks can be affected by such factors as market changes, changes in interest rates, and economic shifts. Shorter cash paybacks also enable companies to recoup an investment sooner and put it to work elsewhere.
- Generally, a payback period of three years or less is desirable; if a project's payback period is less than a year, some contend it should be judged essential.

MORE INFO

See Also:

Return on Investment (pp. 224–226)

Payout Ratio

Dividend cover, and its US equivalent, payout ratio, is a quick reflection of profitability, which is used to evaluate and select investments.

WHAT IT MEASURES

Dividend cover expresses the number of times a company's dividends to common stockholders could be paid out of its net after-tax profits.

Payout ratio expresses the total dividends paid to stockholders as a percentage of a company's net profit in a given period of time.

WHY IT IS IMPORTANT

Whether defined as dividend cover or payout ratio, it measures the likelihood of dividend payments being sustained, and thus is a useful indication of sustained profitability. However, each ratio must be interpreted independently.

A low dividend cover suggests it might be difficult to pay the same level of dividends in a downturn, and that a company is not reinvesting enough in its future. High cover, therefore, implies just the opposite. Negative dividend cover is unusual, and a clear sign of trouble.

The payout ratio, expressed as a percentage or fraction, is an inverse measure: A high ratio indicates a lack of reinvestment in the business, and that current earnings cannot sustain the current dividend payments. In other words, the lower the ratio, the more secure the dividend—and the company's future.

HOW IT WORKS IN PRACTICE

Dividend cover is so named because it shows how many times over the profits could have paid the dividend. If the figure is 3, for example, a firm's profits are three times the level of the dividend paid to shareholders. To calculate dividend cover, divide earnings per share by the dividend per share:

$$\text{Dividend cover} = \frac{\text{Earnings per share}}{\text{Dividend per share}}$$

If a company has earnings per share of $8, and it pays out a dividend of $2.10, dividend cover is:

$$\frac{\$8}{\$2.10} = 3.80$$

An alternative formula divides a company's net profit by the total amount allocated for dividends. So a company that earns $10 million in net profit and allocates $1 million for dividends has a dividend cover of 10, while a company that earns $25 million and pays out $10 million in dividends has a dividend cover of 2.5:

$$\frac{\$10{,}000{,}000}{\$1{,}000{,}000} = 10$$

$$\frac{\$25{,}000{,}000}{\$10{,}000{,}000} = 2.5$$

The payout ratio is calculated by dividing annual dividends paid on common stock by earnings per share:

$$\text{Payout ratio} = \frac{\text{Annual dividend}}{\text{Earnings per share}}$$

Take the company whose earnings per share is $8 and dividend payout is $2.10. Its payout ratio would be:

$$\frac{2.10}{8} = 0.263 = 26.3\%$$

TRICKS OF THE TRADE

- A dividend cover ratio of 2 or higher is usually adequate, and indicates that the dividend is affordable. By the same token, the payout ratio should not exceed two-thirds of earnings. Like most ratios, however, both vary by industry. US real estate investment trusts, for example, pay out almost all their earnings in dividends because US tax laws exempt them from taxes if they do so. American utilities also offer high payout rates.
- A dividend cover ratio below 1.5 is risky, and a ratio below 1 indicates that a company is paying the current year's dividend with retained earnings from a previous year—a practice that cannot continue indefinitely.
- The higher the dividend cover figure, the less likely the dividend will be reduced or eliminated in the future, should profits fall. Companies that suffer sharp declines or outright losses will often continue paying dividends to indicate that their substandard performance is an anomaly.
- On the other hand, a high dividend cover figure may disappoint an investor looking for income, since the figure suggests directors could have declared a larger dividend.
- A high payout ratio clearly appeals to conservative investors seeking income. However, when coupled with weak or falling earnings it could suggest an imminent dividend cut, or that the company is short-changing reinvestment to maintain its payout.
- A payout ratio above 75% is a warning. It suggests the company is failing to reinvest sufficient profits in its business, that the company's earnings are faltering, or that it is trying to attract investors who otherwise would not be interested.
- Newer and faster-growing companies often pay no dividends at all in order to reinvest earnings in the company's development.
- Historically, dividends have provided more than 40% of a stock investor's total portfolio return. However, the figure has been about half that over the last 20 years.

Portfolio Analysis: Duration, Convexity, and Immunization

WHAT THEY MEASURE

Duration is a measure of how sensitive the price of bonds are to changes in interest rates (otherwise known as interest rate risk). For example, if interest rates rise 1%, a bond with a two-year duration will fall about 2% in value. Convexity is a measure of how prices rise when yields fall, and can also be used to measure interest rate risk.

WHY THEY ARE IMPORTANT

Using a combination of duration and convexity allows traders to hedge investments to minimize or offset the impact of changes in interest rates—a process known as immunization.

HOW THEY WORK IN PRACTICE

Duration is a weighted average of the present value of a bond's payments. It provides an insight into how sensitive a bond or portfolio is to changes in interest rates. The longer the duration, the longer the average maturity and, therefore, the bond's sensitivity to interest rate changes. Securities with the same duration have the same interest rate risk exposure. Duration can be expressed in years (to average maturity) or as a percentage (the percentage change in price for a 1% change in its yield to maturity).

$$\text{Duration} = \frac{(P_{-} - P_{+})}{(2 \times P_0 \times \Delta y)}$$

where:

P_0 = bond price

P_{-} = bond price when interest rates are incremented

P_{+} = bond price when rates are decremented

Δy = change in interest rates (decimal form)

Convexity is a measure of the rate at which duration changes as yields fall, and is expressed in squared time (t + 1). To estimate the convexity of a bond or portfolio, we can use the following formula:

$$\text{Convexity approximation} = \frac{(P_+ + P_- - 2P_0)}{2P_0(\Delta y)^2}$$

Immunization: To immunize a portfolio, you need to know the duration of the bonds and adjust the portfolio so the duration is equal to the investment time horizon. For example, you might select bonds that you know will return $10,000 in five years' time regardless of interest rate changes.

Normally, when interest rates go up, bond prices go down. But if a portfolio is immunized, the investor receives a specific rate of return over time regardless of what happens to interest rates, because the portfolio's duration is equal to the investor's time horizon. This means any changes to interest rates will affect the bond's price and reinvestment at the same rate, keeping the rate of return steady. Maintaining an immunized portfolio means rebalancing the portfolio's average duration every time interest rates change, so that the average duration continues to equal the investor's time horizon.

TRICKS OF THE TRADE

- The concept of duration was first developed by Frederick Macaulay in 1938, as a tool for measuring bond price volatility in relation to the length of a bond. However, there are other formulae for calculating duration, including "effective duration" and "modified duration."
- Convexity is usually a positive term, but sometimes the term is negative, such as occurs when a callable bond is nearing its call price. In this case, traders use modified convexity, which is the measured convexity when there is no expected change in future cash flows, or effective convexity, which is the convexity measure for a bond for which future cash flows are expected to change.
- The notion of bond convexity should not be confused with the convexity of the yield curve (see Term Structure of Interest Rates). The latter can assume an arbitrary shape

(although a normal yield curve has negative convexity), and complex stochastic models have been proposed for its evolution.

MORE INFO

Article:

Radcliffe, Brent. "Immunization inoculates against interest rate risk." *Investopedia* (February 26, 2009). Online at: tinyurl.com/5vj7ykk

Website:

This Matter on duration and convexity: thismatter.com/money/bonds/duration-convexity.htm

See Also:

Current Price of a Bond (pp. 90–92)

Price/Earnings Ratio

WHAT IT MEASURES

The price/earnings (P/E) ratio is simply the stock price divided by earnings per share (EPS). While EPS is an actual amount of money, usually expressed in cents per share, the P/E ratio has no units—it is just a number. Thus if a quoted company has a stock price of $100 and EPS of $12 for the last published year, then it has a historical P/E of 8.3. If analysts are forecasting for the next year an EPS of, say, $14 then the forecast P/E is 7.1.

WHY IT IS IMPORTANT

Since EPS is the annual earnings per share of a company, it follows that dividing the stock price by EPS tells us how many years of current EPS are represented by the stock price. In the above example, then, the P/E of 8.3 tells us that investors at the current price are prepared to pay 8.3 years of historical EPS for the stock, or 7.1 years of the forecast next year's EPS. Theoretically, the faster a company is expected to grow, the higher the P/E ratio that investors would award it. It is one measure of how cheap or expensive a stock appears to be.

HOW IT WORKS IN PRACTICE

Forecasts can go wrong, of course, resulting in the infamous profit warnings that are issued by some companies. In these they warn that expected profit targets, for various reasons, will not be met. Understandably, a slump in the stock price is the normal reaction, and analysts would then downgrade their existing forecast EPS. If, in the above example, our forecast of $14 for next year was halved to $7 following a profit warning, the forecast P/E on the same price of $100 would immediately double to 14.3—but in practice the price would usually fall substantially, thus cutting back the forecast P/E.

The P/E ratio is mainly useful in comparisons with other stocks rather than in isolation. For example, if the average P/E in the market is 20, there will be many stocks with P/Es well above and well below this, for a variety of reasons. Similarly, in a particular sector, the P/Es will frequently vary quite widely from the sector average, even though the constituent companies may all be engaged in broadly similar businesses. The reason is that even two businesses doing the same thing will not always be doing it as profitably as each other. One may be far more efficient, as demonstrated by a history of rising EPS compared with the flat EPS picture of the other over a series of years, and the market might recognize this by awarding the more profitable stock a higher P/E.

TRICKS OF THE TRADE

- Take care. The market frequently gets it wrong and many high-P/E stocks have in the past been the most awful long-term investments, losing investors huge amounts of money when the promise of future rapid growth proved to be a chimera. In contrast, many low-P/E companies, often in what are perceived as dull industries, have proved over time to be outstanding investments.
- The P/E is an investment tool that is both invaluable and yet requires extreme caution in its application when comparing and selecting investments. It remains, however, by far the most commonly utilized ratio in investment analysis.

MORE INFO

Book:

Walsh, Ciaran. *Key Management Ratios*. 4th ed. London: FT Prentice Hall, 2008.

See Also:

Earnings per Share (pp. 121–123)
Price/Sales Ratio (pp. 202–203)

Price Elasticity

WHAT IT MEASURES

Price elasticity (sometimes known as price elasticity of demand, or PED) measures how demand for a product or service changes when the price charged is changed.

WHY IT IS IMPORTANT

Price elasticity enables you to predict how sales will be impacted if the price of a product or service is raised. Elasticity measures the responsiveness of consumers to changes in price, and gives businesses a curve to help analyze demand as it relates to price. Businesses can use elasticity to make effective pricing strategies. For example, if demand is inelastic, it may be possible to increase revenues by increasing the price of a product. If demand is elastic, however, businesses would be more likely to invest in advertising to try and build brand loyalty and create inelastic demand.

HOW IT WORKS IN PRACTICE

The basic formula to calculate price elasticity is as follows:

$$\text{Price elasticity} = \frac{\text{Percentage change in quantity demanded}}{\text{Percentage change in price}}$$

To calculate price elasticity on a product that has changed in price from $10 to $12, we need to know the quantity of goods sold at each price. Imagine that at $10, your company sold 150,000 items but at $12, the company sold 110,000 items.

Next, you need to calculate the percentage change in quantity and the percentage change in price. To calculate the percentage change in quantity demanded, use the following calculation:

$$\frac{(\text{New quantity} - \text{Old quantity})}{\text{Old quantity}}$$

So:

$$\frac{(110{,}000 - 150{,}000)}{150{,}000} = \frac{-40}{150} = -0.2667 = -26.67\%$$

While the percentage change in price is calculated as follows:

$$\frac{(\text{New price} - \text{Old price})}{\text{Old price}}$$

So:

$$\frac{(12 - 10)}{12} = \frac{2}{12} = 0.1667 = 16.67\%$$

Using these two figures we calculate the price elasticity as follows:

$$\frac{-26.67\%}{16.67\%} = -1.6$$

We can therefore conclude, ignoring the minus sign as is conventional, the price elasticity of this product, when the price increases from $10 to $12, is 1.6.

TRICKS OF THE TRADE

- When interpreting elasticity figures, the higher the number, the more sensitive consumers are to price changes. A very high figure suggests that if the price goes up, demand for the product or service will fall steeply. A lower figure suggests demand will not be substantially affected by price increases. This type of product is known as "inelastic."
- As a rule of thumb, an inelastic product will have a price elasticity score of one or less. If the elasticity of demand is exactly one, then a small increase or fall in price would result in value of sales remaining steady—the change in volume will exactly balance.

- Sometimes you will find negative elasticity scores (as in the example above)—when prices increase by 10% and sales fall by 20%, the elasticity score would be −2, for example. However, when using elasticity scores, the negative is ignored and expressed simply as the absolute figure "2."
- Elasticity scores change more dramatically over longer periods. This is because people have time to change buying habits over a period of time. Sales might therefore not be affected much by a price increase in year 1, but be significantly impacted by year 3.
- Goods that are elastic tend to be luxury or expensive purchases (cars, holidays, etc) while inelastic goods are those where there are many alternatives available, and which are bought frequently (bread or milk, for example).
- Elasticity is unlikely to be the same across an entire market. Certain firms will always be able to charge above market rates, while others will tend to under-cut the market price to maintain revenues.

MORE INFO

Websites:

Money Terms on price elasticity: moneyterms.co.uk/price-elasticity/

Quick MBA on price elasticity of demand: www.quickmba.com/econ/micro/elas/ped.shtml

Robert Schenk on price elasticity: ingrimayne.com/econ/elasticity/Elastic1.html

See Also:

Elasticity (pp. 131–132)

Price/Sales Ratio

WHAT IT MEASURES

The price/sales (P/S) ratio is another measure, like the price/earnings (P/E) ratio, of the relative value of a stock when compared with others.

WHY IT IS IMPORTANT

Like many such price-based ratios, it does not mean too much in isolation but acquires worth when making comparisons. So a figure of 0.33 does not say a lot on its own, until you start to look at how this matches up to the market average or the sector average, for example.

HOW IT WORKS IN PRACTICE

The P/S ratio is obtained by dividing the market capitalization by the latest published annual sales figure. So a company with a capitalization of $1 billion and sales of $3 billion would have a P/S ratio of 0.33.

P/S will vary with the type of industry. You would expect, for example, that many retailers and other large-scale distributors of goods would have very high sales in relation to their market capitalizations—in other words, a very low P/S. Equally, manufacturers of high-value items would generally have much lower sales figures and thus higher P/S ratios. Like anything to do with share analysis (this being more of an art than a science), it is not always that clear cut ... but that would be the general trend. If you rank companies by ascending P/S, you will usually find that supermarket chains figure among the lowest.

A company with a lower P/S is cheaper than one with a higher ratio, particularly if they are in the same sector so that a direct comparison is appropriate. The lower P/S means that each share of the company is buying you more of its sales than those of the higher P/S company.

Note, though, that it is cheaper only on P/S grounds; that does not mean it is necessarily the more attractive share. There will often be reasons why it has a lower ratio than another, ostensibly similar, company, most commonly because it is less profitable. As far as corporate efficiency goes, this ratio considers only sales, the top line of the profit and loss account. It is a long way from there to the bottom line, the bit that really counts (that is, how much profit the company has made).

TRICKS OF THE TRADE

- A company with a loss would thus still have a P/S ratio, even though it would have no P/E ratio. In consequence, like all investment analysis tools, P/S has to be used with care—but it can be of use for investors. P/S was cited in an extensive study of the New York Stock Exchange as one leading indicator for selecting very long-term shares that perform well.

MORE INFO

Book:

O'Shaughnessy, James. *What Works on Wall Street: The Classic Guide to the Best-Performing Investment Strategies of All Time*. 4th ed. New York: McGraw-Hill, 2011.

See Also:

Price/Earnings Ratio (pp. 197–198)

Quantitative Methods

WHAT THEY ARE

Quantitative methods are a number of statistical and mathematical tools that can be used to capture and analyze information on quantitative data—anything that can be measured or counted.

What differentiates quantitative from qualitative methods is that quantitative methods usually rely on a variation of the scientific method to generate measurable results. Quantitative methods are therefore formulae and models used to generate hypotheses, capture and measure data, or evaluate the results.

WHY THEY ARE IMPORTANT

Imagine you wanted to know whether a particular action would increase the yield of a bond portfolio. If you perform the action once and the yield increases, would you be convinced? If it happened three times consecutively, would you be convinced?

Quantitative methods are used to measure and model outcomes, eliminating rogue results and other influences. Formulating a financial problem or hypothesis into a quantitative model allows us to apply statistical analysis to the problem and calculate the probability of certain outcomes—such as how likely a yield is to increase when a specific action is taken.

For investment managers, quantitative methods are most commonly used to value different classes of securities, analyze criteria for guiding investment decisions, measure risk and asset return, and use statistical techniques for forecasting. They can also be used for calculating yields and prices, frequency distributions, risk and probability, correlation, and regression analysis.

HOW THEY WORK IN PRACTICE

As previously discussed, in finance, quantitative methods are used to perform statistical analysis on a range of financial hypotheses and problems. The first stage in any quantitative method is the development of a theory or hypothesis, against which data can be measured or compared, followed by the application of either descriptive or inferential statistical methods.

Descriptive statistical methods describe properties of the data in front of us, while inferential methods allow us to draw conclusions from data in front of us. For example:

"The average income of the portfolio was $2.8 million per annum over the five-year period" is a descriptive statistic, while "The sample of 50 annual yields from the total portfolio indicates the average income of the portfolio was between $2.6 and $2.9 million per annum," is an inferential statistic.

To test your hypothesis, you might use any of a number of statistical tools, the most common including linear regression. The classical linear regression model (CLRM) is used in finance to estimate unknown parameters using statistical methods. Once you have created regression boundaries you can compute confidence intervals and perform hypothesis testing. An alternative approach is the multiple linear regression model (MLRM), which is used for hypothesis testing in scenarios where there is more than one unknown variable.

Other statistical methods used in quantitative analysis include forecasting tools such as correlation analysis, co-efficiency of correlations, and determination and learning curves.

TRICKS OF THE TRADE

- Although quantitative methods have existed since people first recorded numerical data, the modern idea of quantitative methods has its roots in Auguste Comte's positivist framework.
- Quantitative methods also incorporate the basic principles of statistical interference—the process of making inferences from a small sample about the behavior of a larger population. Two main approaches are estimation and hypothesis testing.

MORE INFO

Books:

Brealey, Richard A., Stewart C. Myers, and Franklin Allen. *Principles of Corporate Finance*. 11th ed. New York: McGraw-Hill, 2013.

Gujarati, Damodar N., and Dawn C. Porter. *Essentials of Econometrics*. 5th ed. New York: McGraw-Hill, 2013.

Oakshott, Les. *Essential Quantitative Methods for Business, Management and Finance*. 5th ed. Basingstoke, UK: Palgrave Macmillan, 2012.

Rate of Return

This may well be as basic and important a computation as there is in finance.

WHAT IT MEASURES

The annual return on an investment, expressed as a percentage of the total amount invested. It also measures the yield of a fixed-income security.

WHY IT IS IMPORTANT

Rate of return is a simple and straightforward way to determine how much investors are being paid for the use of their money, so that they can then compare various investments and select the best—based, of course, on individual goals and acceptable levels of risk.

Rate of return has a second and equally vital purpose: As a common denominator that measures a company's financial performance, for example, in terms of rate of return on assets, equity, or sales.

HOW IT WORKS IN PRACTICE

There is a basic formula that will serve most needs, at least initially:

$$\text{Rate of return} = \frac{(\text{Current value of amount invested} - \text{Original value of amount invested})}{\text{Original value of amount invested}}$$

If $1,000 in capital is invested in stock, and one year later the investment yields $1,100, the rate of return of the investment is calculated like this:

$$\frac{(1100 - 1000)}{1000} = 0.1 = 10\%$$

Now, assume $1,000 is invested again. One year later, the investment grows to $2,000 in value, but after another year the value of the investment falls to $1,200. The rate of return after the first year is:

$$\frac{(2000 - 1000)}{1000} = 1 = 100\%$$

The rate of return after the second year is:

$$\frac{(1200 - 2000)}{2000} = -0.4 = -40\%$$

The average annual return for the two years (also known as average annual arithmetic return) can be calculated using this formula:

$$\text{Average annual return} = \frac{(\text{Rate of return for year 1} + \text{Rate of return for year 2})}{2}$$

Accordingly:

$$\frac{(100\% + -40\%)}{2} = 30\%$$

Be careful, however! The average annual rate of return is a percentage, but one that is accurate over only a short period, so this method should be used accordingly.

The geometric or compound rate of return is a better yardstick for measuring investments over the long run, and takes into account the effects of compounding. As one might expect, this formula is more complex and technical, and beyond the scope of this article.

TRICKS OF THE TRADE

- The real rate of return is the annual return realized on an investment, adjusted for changes in the price due to inflation. If 10% is earned on an investment but inflation is 2%, then the real rate of return is actually 8%.
- Do not confuse rate of return with internal rate of return, which is a more complex calculation.

- Some mutual fund managers have been known to report the average annual rate of return on the investments they manage. In the second example, that figure is 30%, yet the value of the investment is only $200 higher than it was two years ago, or 20%. So, read such reports carefully.

MORE INFO

Book:

Walsh, Ciaran. *Key Management Ratios*. 4th ed. London: FT Prentice Hall, 2008.

See Also:

Expected Rate of Return (pp. 141–142)
Internal Rate of Return (pp. 160–162)
Risk-Adjusted Rate of Return (pp. 231–233)

Reading an Annual Report

GETTING STARTED

Many companies must publish an annual report to its stockholders as a matter of corporate law. The primary purpose of this report is to inform stockholders of the company's performance. As a legal requirement, the report usually contains a profit and loss account, a balance sheet, a cash flow statement, a directors' report, and an auditors' report. The different elements tell you about different aspects of the company's performance and can be read in a particular order to build up a true picture of how it is doing.

Many companies also provide a lot of other nonstatutory information on their affairs, in the interests of general communication. In some cases, this may be little more than gloss, contrived to illustrate the company's wonderful achievements while remaining strangely silent on negative features.

FAQS

Is there any difference between annual reports from private and public companies?

The main difference is usually length. The reports of privately held companies are far shorter because their mandatory reporting requirements are much reduced. Additionally, they are less concerned with image, and consequently will tend to omit the noncompulsory public relations features that are present in public company reports.

What guarantee is there that an annual report is a true picture of a company's performance and not just propaganda put out by directors?

All annual reports have to include a report from the auditors, who are independent accountants charged with investigating a company's financial affairs to ensure that the published figures give a true and fair view of performance. Their investigation cannot extend to examining every single transaction (impossible in a company of any size), so they use statistical sampling and other risk-based testing procedures to assess the quality of the company's systems as a basis for producing the annual report. They are not infallible, but they stand between the stockholders and the directors as a way of trying to ensure probity in the running of a company.

MAKING IT HAPPEN

Understanding the Main Contents of an Annual Report

The best way to look at this is to take an example. Standard sections in annual reports can vary from country to country, but the following is the contents list of the annual report of a medium-sized US public company—let's call it X Inc.

- X World;
- Chairman's Statement;
- Chief Executive's Review;
- Financial Review;
- Board of Directors;
- Board Report on Remuneration;
- Directors' Responsibilities;
- Report of the Auditors;
- Financial Statements;
- Five-Year Record;
- Stockholder Information.

Here's what each of these sections is about:

X World: Belongs in the PR area. It tells you about the company, its products and markets.

Chairman's Statement: Comments on the group results for the year and on future developments. It also provides detail on earnings per share and dividends.

Chief Executive's Review: Goes into more detail about individual divisions, breaking down the operating results from areas around the world. It tells us a bit about discontinued businesses and new ones acquired.

Financial Review: Expands on the two previous sections in a more quantitative way, looking at things like cash flow and how it affected group debt; interest charges; the effect of exchange rate fluctuations on profits, assets and liabilities; exceptional items that affect the profits (such as the disposal of a subsidiary company), and so on.

Board of Directors: Lists the directors, with a brief description and photo of each.

Board Report on Remuneration: Describes the work of a committee of nonexecutive directors, who decide the directors' income and that of other senior employees. Their remit includes looking at service contracts, bonus and stock option plans, plus pension plans. It includes an analysis of the pay of each director, with comparable figures for the previous year, plus details of stock options, and so on.

Directors' Responsibilities: A mandatory statement showing exactly what the directors are obliged to discharge with regard to the annual report, maintaining accurate accounting records, and so on.

Report of the Auditors: This is simply what it says. Their findings are published using standard language.

Financial Statements: These are the main purpose of the annual report. In the example of X Inc., they consist of:

- *Consolidated Profit and Loss Account.* The profit and loss account of all the group as one consolidated account.
- *Consolidated and Company Balance Sheets.* The former is the group balance sheet and the latter is for the parent company alone.
- *Consolidated Cash Flow Statement.* A guide to how the money flowing in and out of the company was utilized.
- *Management's Responsibility for Financial Reporting.*
- *Management's Discussion and Analysis.*
- *Notes to the Financial Statements.* These amplify numerous points contained in the figures and are usually critical for anyone wishing to study the financial statements in detail.

Five-Year Record: Shows a very abbreviated set of profit and loss and balance sheet figures for the current and previous four years. Some companies provide a 10-year record.

Stockholder Information: Deals with matters such as the registered office, stockholder registrars, brokers, lawyers, dates for meetings and dividend payments, and other points.

Choosing the Right Order in which to Read the Report

One way is simply to read the report from cover to cover, like a book. However, if you are not experienced with these things, that may lead you to giving equal weight to all the contents and, perhaps, overvaluing the glossy PR bits at the expense of the hard facts shown by the figures.

Start with the Auditors' Report

Remember that this thin gray line of accountants is all that stands between the outside stockholder and the directors. To speed up matters, look at the final paragraph—their opinion. Does that statement give a true and fair view? If so, fine. If not, then it is said to be "qualified." Qualifications vary in depth from the disastrous, meaning that the company has gotten something seriously wrong, to perhaps a difference of opinion between the auditors and the board over some accounting matter. Most auditors' reports are unqualified, but, if there is a qualification present, you will have to judge how much the financial statements can be relied upon as a measure of the company's performance.

Next, Turn to the Five/Ten-Year Review

This is where you build up a mental picture of the company's financial history. Look at earnings per share (EPS)—is it increasing, decreasing, fluctuating wildly? This gives you an idea of how it has been doing over the period. Look at dividends, if any, and consider their pattern. Do they follow EPS or, as is likely, are they showing a smoother picture? Look at company debt, if the information is there, and compare it with stockholders' funds. How is it changing over the years?

Generally, try to build up a view as to whether the company is doing better, worse, or perhaps has no particular pattern over the period. Depending on your reasons for reading the report, a set of prejudices will have begun to develop from this historical picture. If it shows a declining financial situation, this could be a good thing from some points of view—if you wish to acquire the company, for example. If you are an employee though, it would not be very encouraging. So reading reports depends to some extent on which angle you are coming from.

Now Read the Chairman's and Directors' Comments

These will give a deeper feel for the company's business, over and above the raw numerical data. Try to exercise a degree of skepticism in some areas, because it is natural for directors to attempt to play up the good points and play down the less good ones.

Get to the Heart of the Matter

The kernel of the report is the Financial Statements and the huge number of notes that accompany them. A lot of it is in highly technical accounting terminology, but it gives you the intimate financial detail on the year. Never ignore the notes—they are critical. In fact some investment analysts read the report from the back, because the notes are so important.

Notes have increased dramatically over the years as new legal and accounting standards have been introduced, primarily to enforce standardization so that financial reports are more comparable, but also to avoid "creative accounting," whereby some companies have tried to conceal (legitimately) financially undesirable situations.

Relax with the Glossy Stuff

Having absorbed all that really matters, settle back and read the glossy parts that tell you how wonderful the company is. Just remember to exercise a mild degree of cynicism here—this is the least important, though no doubt the most visually attractive, part of the annual report. The real picture of the company is the numbers, not the photo of the guy in the hard hat standing on an oil rig!

A Common Mistake

Don't pay too much attention to pretty pictures and directors' comments and too little to the accounting data.

This can give a false view of how well, or badly, the company is doing. Understandably, many people have difficulty in comprehending the figures. But if you want to appreciate annual reports properly, then learning to read financial reports is essential.

Some cynics among investment analysts have even expressed the view that there is an inverse relationship between the number of glossy pages in an annual report and the company's actual performance. Maybe that's a little harsh. . .but there might be something in it.

MORE INFO

Websites:

Financial Reporting Council's (FRC; UK) accounting and reporting policy: tinyurl.com/d5qtysr

Securities and Exchange Commission (SEC; US): www.sec.gov

Reserve Ratio

Also called the "reserve requirement," the reserve ratio is a device used both to facilitate financial stability and to influence credit conditions.

WHAT IT MEASURES

In the United Kingdom and in certain European countries there is no compulsory ratio, although banks will have their own internal measures and targets to be able to repay customer deposits as they forecast they will be required. In the United States the policy is more prescriptive, and specified percentages of deposits—specified by the Federal Reserve Board—must be kept by banks in a noninterest-bearing account at one of the 12 Federal Reserve Banks located throughout the country.

WHY IT IS IMPORTANT

To provide stability. In view of the volume and unpredictability of transactions that clear through their accounts every day, banks and financial depositories must maintain a cushion of funds to protect themselves against debits that could leave their accounts overdrawn at the end of the day, and thus subject to penalty.

As a result of the creation of reserve ratios, periods of financial stress are no longer characterized by runs on banks by depositors.

HOW IT WORKS IN PRACTICE

In Europe, the reserve requirement of an institution is calculated by multiplying the reserve ratio for each category of items in the reserve base, set by the European Central Bank, with the amount of those items in the institution's balance sheets. These figures vary according to the institution.

The required reserve ratio in the United States is set by federal law, and depends on the amount of checkable deposits a bank holds. The first $44.3 million of deposits are subject to a 3% reserve requirement. Deposits in excess of $44.3 million are subject to a 10% reserve requirement. These breakpoints are reviewed annually in accordance with money supply growth. No reserves are required against certificates of deposit or savings accounts.

The reserve ratio requirement limits a bank's lending to a certain fraction of its demand deposits. The current rule allows a bank to issue loans to an amount equal to 90% of such deposits, holding 10% in reserve. The reserves can be held in any combination of vault cash and deposit at a Federal Reserve Bank.

A bank facing a reserve deficiency has several options. It can try to borrow reserves for one or more days from another bank, sell marketable assets such as government securities, or bid for funds in the money market, such as large certificates of deposit (CDs) or eurodollars. As a last resort, it can pledge collateral and borrow at the Federal Reserve's discount window.

In order to meet deposit withdrawal contingencies, many banks maintain a margin of excess reserves above the required reserve ratio, since the required reserves are really not available to meet withdrawal liquidity needs. Excess reserves are higher than those needed to meet reserve and clearing requirements, and provide extra protection against overdrafts and deficiencies in required reserves.

TRICKS OF THE TRADE

- Because reserves earn no interest, they have an adverse effect on bank earnings.
- In practice, the required reserve ratio has been adjusted only infrequently by the US Federal Reserve Board.
- US depository institutions hold required reserves in one of two forms: vault cash on hand at the bank or—more significant for monetary policy—required reserve balances in accounts with the Reserve Bank for their respective Federal Reserve District.

Residual Value

WHAT IT MEASURES

Residual value is the value an asset will have after it has been depreciated, or amortized. Residual value is sometimes referred to as "salvage" value.

WHY IT IS IMPORTANT

According to international financial reporting standards, residual value is the value an asset should have if it is in the expected condition at the end of its useful life, after the cost of selling it.

HOW IT WORKS IN PRACTICE

When calculating the residual value of a business asset, the salvage value is used in conjunction with the purchase price and accounting methods to determine the amount by which the asset depreciates each period. For example, with a straight-line basis, an asset that cost $5,000 and has a salvage value of $1,000 and a useful life of five years would be depreciated at $800 ([5,000 − 1,000] ÷ 5) each year.

This straight-line method uses the following formula to calculate residual value:

$$\text{Depreciation expense} = \frac{(\text{Cost of fixed asset} - \text{Scrap value})}{\text{Lifespan}}$$

An alternative approach is to use the declining-balance method, which assumes that an asset loses value more rapidly in the early part of its useful lifetime. In the case of machinery, this is often a more realistic approach. To calculate residual value using this methodology, each period of depreciation is based on the previous year's net book value, estimated lifespan, and a factor of 2 (known as the double-declining balance). For example:

$$\text{Depreciation expense} = \text{Previous period NBV} \times \frac{\text{Factor}}{\text{N}}$$

For the double-declining balance method, using the vehicle example from above, we compute the depreciation after the first year:

$$17000 \times \frac{2}{5} = \$6800$$

In business accounting there are three common methods of calculating the residual value of a business:

1 Perpetuity business valuation: Using this methodology, the business assumes the company's future cash flow will continue indefinitely, and the residual value of the asset is calculated according to the following formula:

$$\text{Residual value} = \frac{\text{Free cash flow in year } n}{r}$$

where r is the discount rate and n is the last year of the analysis period.

2 Liquidation business valuation: Using this methodology assumes the most conservative way to calculate residual value is to assume the asset will be liquidated at the end of the forecasting period. So, residual value is calculated as being the net liquidation value—the asset's value (including cash, inventory, plant) less liabilities. This value is discounted for the beginning of the period, before adding it to the discounted cash flow, to calculate the company's value.

3 Price earnings valuation: Assumes the best way to determine a venture's residual value is to calculate its market price using the relevant price earning factor as follows:

$$\text{Residual value} = \frac{\text{Net profit in year } n \times \text{Comparative PE}}{r}$$

where r is the discount rate and n is the selected year. Comparative PE refers to the PE of any similar company, or the industry average.

The result is then discounted to the beginning of the plan period and added to discounted cash flow.

TRICKS OF THE TRADE

- Residual values should be reviewed annually alongside the useful life of assets, and depreciation adjusted if the residual value of an asset has changed.
- Intangible assets have a zero residual value. Some tangible assets may also have a zero residual value if they cannot be resold, or if there are costs associated with their disposal that outstrip the residual value.
- Residual values used for calculating depreciation should be calculated per asset, but most companies would simplify the calculations by grouping together items into categories.
- Residual value can be built into leases. The residual value of leased assets is the cost of the asset minus less repayments of capital made over the lifetime of the lease.

MORE INFO

Article:

White, Diane. "Depreciation of fixed assets: Straight line, units-of-production, and double declining method." *Suite101.com* (September 15, 2008). Online at: tinyurl.com/5w6625f

Website:

Money Terms on residual value: moneyterms.co.uk/residual-value/

See Also:

Depreciation (pp. 105–110)

Return on Assets

Return on assets—or simply ROA—may also be termed return on total assets (ROTA) or return on net assets (RONA). Whatever its designation, it is often referred to as the No. 1 ratio in finance.

WHAT IT MEASURES

A company's profitability, expressed as a percentage of its total assets.

WHY IT IS IMPORTANT

Return on assets measures how effectively a company has used the total assets at its disposal to generate earnings. Because the ROA formula reflects total revenue, total cost, and assets deployed, the ratio itself reflects a management's ability to generate income during the course of a given period, usually a year.

Naturally, the higher the return, the better the profit performance. ROA is a convenient way of comparing a company's performance with that of its competitors, although the items on which the comparison is based may not always be identical.

HOW IT WORKS IN PRACTICE

To calculate ROA, divide a company's net income by its total assets, then multiply by 100 to express the figure as a percentage:

$$\text{Return on assets} = \frac{\text{Net income}}{\text{Total assets}}$$

If net income is $30, and total assets are $420, the ROA is:

$$\frac{30}{420} = 0.0714 = 7.14\%$$

A variation of this formula can be used to calculate return on net assets (RONA):

$$\text{Return on net assets} = \frac{\text{Net income}}{(\text{Fixed assets} + \text{Working capital})}$$

And, on occasion, the formula will separate after-tax interest expense from net income:

$$\text{Return on assets} = \frac{(\text{Net income} + \text{Interest expense})}{\text{Total assets}}$$

It is therefore important to understand what each component of the formula actually represents.

TRICKS OF THE TRADE

- Some experts recommend using the net income value at the end of the given period, and the assets' value from the beginning of the period, or an average value taken over the complete period, rather than an end-of-the-period value; otherwise, the calculation will include assets that have accumulated during the year, which can be misleading.
- While a high ratio indicates a greater return, it must still be balanced against such factors as risk, sustainability, and reinvestment in the business through development costs. Some managements will sacrifice the long-term interests of investors in order to achieve an impressive ROA in the short term.
- A climbing return on assets usually indicates a climbing stock price, because it tells investors that a management is skilled at generating profits from the resources that a business owns.
- Acceptable ROAs vary by sector. In banking, for example, a ROA of 1% or better is a considered to be the standard benchmark of superior performance.
- ROA is an effective way of measuring the efficiency of manufacturers, but can be suspect when measuring service companies, or companies whose primary assets are people.
- Other variations of the ROA formula do exist.

MORE INFO

See Also:

Asset Turnover (pp. 26–28)
Asset Utilization (pp. 29–31)

Return on Investment

Return on investment (ROI) is a ratio that is used frequently—perhaps too frequently. Its definition can vary widely. Indeed, ROI today is not only a family of measurements of the performance of invested capital but also a concept, one used to justify expenditure on almost everything.

WHAT IT MEASURES

In the financial realm, the overall profit or loss on an investment expressed as a percentage of the total amount invested or total funds appearing on a company's balance sheet.

WHY IT IS IMPORTANT

Like return on assets or return on equity, return on investment measures a company's profitability and its management's ability to generate profits from the funds investors have placed at its disposal.

One opinion holds that if a company's operations cannot generate net earnings at a rate that exceeds the cost of borrowing funds from financial markets, the future of that company is grim.

HOW IT WORKS IN PRACTICE

The most basic expression of ROI can be found by dividing a company's net profit (also called net earnings) by the total investment (total debt plus total equity), then multiplying by 100 to arrive at a percentage:

$$\text{Return on investment} = \frac{\text{Net profit}}{\text{Total investment}}$$

If, say, net profit is $30 and total investment is $250, the ROI is:

$$\frac{30}{250} = 0.12 = 12\%$$

A more complex variation of ROI is an equation known as the Du Pont formula:

$$ROI = \frac{\text{Net profit after taxes}}{\text{Total assets}} = \frac{\text{Net profit after taxes}}{\text{Sales}} \times \frac{\text{Sales}}{\text{Total assets}}$$

If, for example, net profit after taxes is $30, total assets are $250, and sales are $500, then:

$$\frac{30}{250} = \frac{30}{500} \times \frac{500}{250} = 12\% = 6\% \times 2 = 12\%$$

Champions of this formula, which was developed by the Du Pont Company in the 1920s, say that it helps to reveal how a company has both deployed its assets and controlled its costs, and how it can achieve the same percentage return in different ways.

For stockholders, the variation of the basic ROI formula used by investors is:

$$ROI = \frac{(\text{Net income} + \text{Current value} - \text{Original value})}{\text{Original value}}$$

If, for example, somebody invests $5,000 in a company and a year later has earned $100 in dividends, while the value of the stock is $5,200, the return on investment would be:

$$\frac{(100 + 5{,}200 - 5{,}000)}{5{,}000} = \frac{300}{5{,}000} = 0.06 = 6\%$$

TRICKS OF THE TRADE

- Securities investors can use yet another ROI formula: net income divided by common stock and preferred stock equity plus long-term debt.
- It is vital to understand exactly what a return on investment measures—for example, assets, equity, or sales. Without this

understanding, comparisons may be misleading or suspect. A search for "return on investment" on the internet, for example, harvests everything from staff training to e-commerce to advertising and promotions!

- Be sure to establish whether the net profit figure used is before or after provision for taxes. This is important for making ROI comparisons accurate.

MORE INFO

See Also:

Payback Period (pp. 188–190)

Return on Sales

Although return on sales (ROS) is another tool used to analyze profitability, it is perhaps a better indication of efficiency. In some business environments, it is also called margin on sales percentage, or net margin.

WHAT IT MEASURES

A company's operating profit or loss as a percentage of total sales for a given period, typically a year.

WHY IT IS IMPORTANT

Return on sales (ROS) shows how efficiently management uses the sales dollar, thus reflecting its ability to manage costs and overheads and operate efficiently. It also indicates a company's ability to withstand adverse conditions such as falling prices, rising costs, or declining sales. The higher the figure, the better a company is able to endure price wars and falling prices.

Return on sales can be useful in assessing the annual performances of cyclical companies that may have no earnings during particular months, and of companies whose business requires a huge capital investment and thus incurs substantial amounts of depreciation.

HOW IT WORKS IN PRACTICE

The calculation is very basic:

$$\text{Return on sales} = \frac{\text{Operating profit}}{\text{Total sales}}$$

So, if a company earns $30 on sales of $400, its return on sales is:

$$\frac{30}{400} = 0.075 = 7.5\%$$

TRICKS OF THE TRADE

- While easy to grasp, return on sales has its limits, since it sheds no light on the overall cost of sales or the four factors that contribute to it: Materials, labor, production overheads, and administrative and selling overheads.
- Some calculations use operating profit before subtracting interest and taxes; others use after-tax income. Either figure is acceptable as long as ROS comparisons are consistent. Obviously, using income before interest and taxes will produce a higher ratio.
- The ratio's operating profit figure may also include special allowances and extraordinary nonrecurring items, which, in turn, can inflate the percentage and be misleading.
- The ratio varies widely by industry. The supermarket business, for example, is heavily dependent on volume and usually has a low return on sales.
- Return on sales remains of special importance to retail sales organizations, which can compare their respective ratios with those of competitors and industry norms.

Return on Stockholders' Equity

Return on equity (ROE) is probably the most widely used measure of how well a company is performing for its stockholders.

WHAT IT MEASURES

Profitability, specifically the percentage return that was delivered to a company's owners.

WHY IT IS IMPORTANT

ROE is a fundamental indication of a company's ability to increase its earnings per share and thus the quality of its stock, because it reveals how well a company is using its money to generate additional earnings.

It is a relatively straightforward benchmark, easy to calculate, and is applicable to a majority of industries. ROE allows investors to compare a company's use of their equity with other investments, and to compare the performance of companies in the same industry. ROE can also help to evaluate trends in a business.

Businesses that generate high returns on equity are businesses that pay off their stockholders handsomely and create substantial assets for each dollar invested.

HOW IT WORKS IN PRACTICE

To calculate ROE, divide the net income shown on the income statement (usually of the past year) by stockholders' equity, which appears on the balance sheet:

$$\text{Return on equity} = \frac{\text{Net income}}{\text{Owners' equity}}$$

For example, if net income is $450 and equity is $2,500, then:

$$\frac{450}{2{,}500} = 0.18 = 18\%$$

TRICKS OF THE TRADE

- Because new variations of the ROE ratio do appear, it is important to know how the figure is calculated.
- Return on equity for most companies certainly should be in the double digits; investors often look for 15% or higher, while a return of 20% or more is considered excellent.
- Seasoned investors also review five-year average ROE, to gauge consistency.
- A word of caution: Financial statements usually report assets at book value, which is the purchase price minus depreciation; they do not show replacement costs. A business with older assets should show higher rates of ROE than a business with newer assets.
- Examining ROE with return on assets can indicate if a company is debt-heavy. If a company has very little debt, it is reasonable to assume that its management is earning high profits and/or using assets effectively.
- A high ROE also could be due to leverage (a method of corporate funding in which a higher proportion of funds is raised through borrowing than issuing stock). If liabilities are high the balance sheet will reveal it, hence the need to review it.

MORE INFO

Book:

Walsh, Ciaran. *Key Management Ratios*. 4th ed. London: FT Prentice Hall, 2008.

See Also:

Dividend Yield (pp. 116–118)
Earnings per Share (pp. 121–123)

Risk-Adjusted Rate of Return

Knowing an investment's risk-adjusted return goes a long way toward determining just how much "bang for the buck" is really being generated.

WHAT IT MEASURES

How much an investment returned in relation to the risk that was assumed to attain it.

WHY IT IS IMPORTANT

Being able to compare a high-risk, potentially high-return investment with a low-risk, lower-return investment helps to answer a key question that confronts every investor: Is it worth the risk?

By itself, the historical average return of an investment, asset, or portfolio can be quite misleading and a faulty indicator of future performance. Risk-adjusted return is a much better barometer.

The calculation also helps to reveal whether the returns of the portfolio reflect smart investment decisions, or the taking on of excess risk that may or may not have been worth what was gained. This is particularly helpful in appraising the performance of money managers.

HOW IT WORKS IN PRACTICE

There are several ways to calculate risk-adjusted return. Each has its strengths and shortcomings. All require particular data, such as an investment's rate of return, the risk-free return rate for a given period (usually the performance of a 90-day US Treasury bill over 36 months), and a market's performance and its standard deviation.

Which one to use? It often depends on an investor's focus, principally whether the focus is on upside gains or downside losses.

Perhaps the most widely used is the **Sharpe ratio**. This measures the potential impact of return volatility on expected return and the amount of return earned per unit of risk. The higher a fund's Sharpe ratio, the better its historical risk-adjusted performance, and the higher the number the greater the return per unit of risk. The formula is:

$$\text{Sharpe ratio} = \frac{(\text{Portfolio return} - \text{Risk-free return})}{\text{Standard deviation of portfolio return}}$$

Take, for example, two investments, one returning 54%, the other 26%. At first glance, the higher figure clearly looks the better choice, but because of its high volatility it has a Sharpe ratio of 0.279, while the investment with a lower return has a ratio of 0.910. On a risk-adjusted basis the latter would be the wiser choice.

The **Treynor ratio** also measures the excess of return per unit of risk. Its formula is:

$$\text{Treynor ratio} = \frac{(\text{Portfolio return} - \text{Risk-free return})}{\text{Portfolio's beta}}$$

In this formula (and others that follow), beta is a separately calculated figure that describes the tendency of an investment to respond to marketplace swings. The higher the beta, the greater the volatility, and vice versa.

A third formula, **Jensen's measure**, is often used to rate a money manager's performance against a market index, and whether or not an investment's risk was worth its reward. The formula is:

$$\text{Jensen's measure} = \text{Portfolio return} - \text{Risk-free return} - \text{Portfolio beta} \times (\text{Benchmark return} - \text{Risk-free return})$$

TRICKS OF THE TRADE

- A fourth formula, the **Sortino ratio**, also exists. Its focus is more on downside risk than potential opportunity, and its calculation is more complex.
- There are no benchmarks for these values. In order to be useful the numbers should be compared with the ratios of other investments.

- No single measure is perfect, so experts recommend using them broadly. For instance, if a particular investment class is on a roll and does not experience a great deal of volatility, a good return per unit of risk does not necessarily reflect management genius. When the overall momentum of technology stocks drove returns straight up in 1999, Sharpe ratios climbed with them, and did not reflect any of the sector's volatility that was to erupt in late 2000.
- Most of these measures can be used to rank the risk-adjusted performance of individual stocks, various portfolios over the same time, and mutual funds with similar objectives.

MORE INFO

See Also:

Sharpe Ratio (pp. 237–238)
Treynor Ratio (pp. 260–261)

Scenario Analysis

WHAT IT MEASURES

Businesses have always planned for "what if" scenarios—and based their decision-making on likely future events. Scenario analysis is simply a formal tool to model the likelihood of various scenarios and their outcomes. Scenario analysis has been widely used in asset management and risk management since the 1970s, to analyze interest rate risks. However, it can be applied to a wide set of corporate and financial activities, including equity prices, exchange rates, commodity prices, and volatility of prices.

WHY IT IS IMPORTANT

Scenario analysis helps companies and investors to measure the expected value of an investment. By combining this information with probability, analysts can make highly accurate predictions about the likelihood of realizing the expected value. Comparing the probability distribution of an event is equivalent to calculating the risk of an investment and important for the same reason—it allows you to make better decisions about business and financial investments.

There are many different approaches to scenario analysis, but one common method is to determine the high/low spread and standard deviation from daily or monthly returns, then compute the value of the portfolio if each security generated returns two or three basis points above and below this average.

This method means the investor or company can have reasonable certainty that the value of a portfolio will remain within expected parameters over a given period of time.

HOW IT WORKS IN PRACTICE

A typical use of scenario analysis would be to consider what happens to the value of a security if interest rates fell, remained static, or increased.

The first step is to consider all the possible outcomes, or paths, that will be taken by relevant risk factors (in this case, interest rates). Each potential outcome is considered over the same time period. In the simple example below, we can see all the relevant outcomes that might be affected by a 100 basis point fall in interest rates, followed by 24 months of static rates:

Time (months)	1-month LIBOR	3-month LIBOR	6-month LIBOR	12-month LIBOR	COFI
0	3.11	3.79	3.84	4.00	3.54
6	2.11	2.79	3.84	4.00	3.54
12	2.11	2.79	3.84	4.00	3.54
18	2.11	2.79	3.84	4.00	3.54
24	2.11	2.79	3.84	4.00	3.54

Once you have identified the scenario, the next step is to project what happens for each of these rates at the given point in time. This extrapolation may be relatively simple, showing the cost of debt in each scenario, or might be more complex—for example, by incorporating other financial data to produce a cash flow forecast, or value at risk metric.

TRICKS OF THE TRADE

- Scenario analysis allows analysts to plan for their "worst-case scenario." Being able to quantify the potential costs of a possible outcome is vital in risk management and forming business strategy. Scenario planning can be highly detailed, and customized to accommodate any number of variables, such as the flattening of the yield curve or narrowing spreads.
- One advantage of scenario analysis is that it is simple to use and very flexible. It can address almost any present or future risk, and can anticipate the impact of future business decisions. However, its major drawback is that it can only consider the impact of risks that are anticipated—outputs are entirely limited to paths suggested by the user, and so if you overlook a risk, it will not be calculated.
- It is also important to remember that if scenario analysis is based on probability, there is still a potential that the low and high extreme values could occur. This is why scenario analysis is often

run alongside risk analysis to determine whether these potential risks are within acceptable tolerance levels.

- When dealing with complex scenarios over multiple time periods and involving many possible outcomes (such as the impact on 1,000 clients of 100 different interest rate permutations) scenario analysis can be extremely cumbersome, generating large and complex tables. In such instances, duration analysis can provide more user-friendly analysis.
- Another alternative is to use scenario analysis and the Monte Carlo method, to calculate results based on a large number of random scenarios. This approach is sometimes also referred to as "simulation analysis."

MORE INFO

Website:

Mind Tools on scenario analysis: www.mindtools.com/pages/article/newSTR_98.htm

Sharpe Ratio

WHAT IT MEASURES

The Sharpe ratio, devised in 1966 by economist William F. Sharpe, measures the ratio of return from a portfolio to volatility. It is used to compare and select investment options, and identify which portfolio offers the most risk-efficient investment.

WHY IT IS IMPORTANT

The Sharpe ratio provides a simple way compare two assets with the same expected return—showing which will give the greatest return given an equal level of risk. The key advantage of the Sharpe ratio is that it can be easily calculated without needing any additional data regarding the asset's profitability.

HOW IT WORKS IN PRACTICE

The Sharpe ratio is calculated by subtracting the risk-free rate from the return of the portfolio, then dividing by the standard deviation of the portfolio. To use the Sharpe ratio, apply the following formula:

$$\text{Sharpe ratio} = \frac{(\text{Expected rate of return} - \text{Risk-free rate})}{\text{Standard deviation of the portfolio}}$$

The higher the Sharpe ratio, the better the return for each unit of risk. How does this work in practice?

Imagine that portfolio A generates a return of 15%, while portfolio B generates a return of just 12%. It would seem at first glance that portfolio A has performed better. However, if portfolio A was much riskier then it may be the case that B has a better risk-adjusted rate of return.

If we imagine the risk-free rate in this scenario is 5% and the portfolios have standard deviations of 8% and 5% respectively, then we can see that portfolio A would have a Sharpe ratio of 1.25, while portfolio B would have a Sharpe ratio of 1.4. This suggests that, adjusted for risk, portfolio B presents the better investment.

TRICKS OF THE TRADE

- When using the Sharpe ratio, a score of 1 or better is considered good. A ratio above 2 is considered very good, and 3 would be considered excellent.
- Using the Sharpe ratio doesn't always provide an accurate analysis of return on risk or volatility. This is because portfolio standard deviation can reflect upside or downside returns—and the ratio does not differentiate between these outcomes. Some analysts argue that using standard deviation to measure volatility is not strictly effective, since standard deviation is not a measure of volatility. Instead, standard deviation is really a rough proxy for concepts such as "risk."
- When using the Sharpe ratio, it is wise to adjust the ratio for portfolio analysis. If you are comparing two potential investments for portfolios, then the ratio may not be accurate if one investment is highly correlated with other investments in the portfolio. The solution is therefore to use different Sharpe ratios for different portfolios.
- The Sharpe ratio is unusual in that it can be applied to both ex-ante (expected) returns and ex-poste (historical) returns.

MORE INFO

Article:

Sharpe, William F. "The Sharpe ratio." *Journal of Portfolio Management* (Fall 1994). Online at: www.stanford.edu/~wfsharpe/art/sr/sr.htm

Website:

Hedge Funds Consistency Index on Sharpe ratio: www.hedgefund-index.com/d_sharpe.asp

See Also:

Risk-Adjusted Rate of Return (pp. 231–233)
Treynor Ratio (pp. 260–261)

Statistical Process Control Methods

WHAT IT MEASURES

Statistical Process Control (SPC) is a tool for monitoring and controlling variation in processes such as manufacturing of goods, testing, or statistical results. It was created in the 1920s by Dr W. Edwards Deming, who claimed the majority of variation was due to operator over-adjustment. SPC requires an organization to:

- determine the process parameters that need to be monitored;
- create a control chart to confirm the process is under control;
- collect data to compare with the control chart to identify process variation.

WHY IT IS IMPORTANT

SPC itself doesn't improve your processes—it can only tell you if variation has increased beyond normal levels. However, this information enables businesses to incorporate or eliminate the changes causing an abnormal variation. This is important because it provides an understanding of business baselines, gives insights into possible process improvements, and shows the value and results of existing processes. SPC can also provide real-time analysis to establish where business processes can be improved, improving decision-making.

HOW IT WORKS IN PRACTICE

The key tool in applying SPC is the control chart that illustrates what a process looks like (statistically) when it is in-control. Control charts typically measure variable data and monitor the process target (mean result) and process range. There are a number of different sorts of control chart but among the most common are the X¯ chart (pronounced "x bar" but also known as the averages or means chart), and the R chart (also known as the range chart).

This type of control chart has three key elements: a center line, an upper control limit, and a lower control limit. The center line on an X¯ control chart is the process mean, while the center line on an R chart is the mean range.

The upper and lower control limits (UCL and LCL) are set to represent deviation from the mean that includes 99.7% of all data points (i.e., plus and minus 3 standard deviations from the mean). Data is then collected from the process and the mean plotted on the X^- and R charts—which can be interpreted to determine if the process is staying in-control or is out-of-control.

In the example below, a company is manufacturing pencils that are 16mm in diameter (mean), and they want to know if the process is in-control, and the level of variation in the pencils created.

The company begins by collecting a series of sample measurements, which are placed in subgroups. Next, the mean of each subgroup is calculated by adding all the measurements together and dividing by the number of measurements in the subgroup.

Next, the company calculates the mean of all of the means—this gives an overall mean for the data. This overall mean is the centre line in the control chart—in our example this is 13.75.

Next, the company must calculate S, the standard deviation of the data points. This can be easily calculated in Excel using the formula =STDEV (data points).

Next, calculate the UCL and LCL as follows:

$$UCL = CL + 3 \times S$$
$$LCL = CL - 3 \times S$$

where CL is the center line or overall mean value. Draw a line on the control chart to represent the UCL and LCL.

On your X^- chart, the x-axis shows the subgroup means from your original calculation. The y-axis represents actual measurements from the process over time. As a rule of thumb, the process is considered out-of-control if any point falls beyond the UCL or LCL lines (i.e., more than 3 standard deviations from the mean).

Control charts may also indicate a process is out-of-control if eight consecutive points fall on the same side of the center line, or if more than two consecutive points are more than one standard deviation point from the mean.

TRICKS OF THE TRADE

- Using a spreadsheet application, it is possible to calculate standard deviation and mean for a set of data. In Excel this is done using the STDEV and AVERAGE functions.
- The benefits of SPC won't be immediately realized in every organization. SPC is best applied where there are clearly defined and consistent processes, and where the organization's leadership is willing to identify and address new problems that might be identified by SPC.

MORE INFO

Books:

Oakland, John. *Statistical Process Control*. 6th ed. Amsterdam: Elsevier Butterworth-Heinemann, 2008.

Stapenhurst, Tim. *Mastering Statistical Process Control: A Handbook for Performance Improvement Using SPC Cases*. Amsterdam: Elsevier Butterworth-Heinemann, 2005.

Website:

MiC Quality SPC course: www.margaret.net/spc/

Stochastic Modeling

WHAT IT MEASURES

Stochastic modeling uses thousands of simulations to produce probability distributions for various outcomes. It is widely used to predict how stock markets, bonds, and gilts will perform in the future.

WHY IT IS IMPORTANT

Advocates of stochastic modeling argue that randomness is a fundamental characteristic of financial markets. While some agents may be more successful at predicting future trends than others, modeling the likely outcome of investment activities must take account of probability, and particularly the risk of random events negatively impacting investments.

Many investment tools are "deterministic" in that they are clockwork systems which, given the same starting conditions, will generate exactly the same answer. This approach is not perfect when applied to financial markets, where there is an important element of chance, specifically relating to volatility and distribution.

Stochastic modeling provides a structured way of looking at a portfolio, taking into account random factors such as inflation or risk tolerance. If modeling shows a low probability of reaching investment goals, the fund can be diversified or contribution levels altered.

HOW IT WORKS IN PRACTICE

Stochastic modeling relies upon Monte Carlo simulation to generate random numbers upon which a stochastic formula is applied. This shows what impact specific random events will have on the distribution of probable outcomes.

For example, imagine you wanted to calculate the probability that a million door handles manufactured using four key parts would be too short or long to be used. You would have a million of each of the four different parts, and randomly select the parts to assemble each handle.

To calculate the probability, you would define a range of measurements for each part, and simulate what happens when randomly selected parts are put together. Of course, this is not something that could be calculated manually. Instead, a stochastic model would calculate thousands of probable outcomes based on a large number of random simulations, reflecting the random variation of combinations.

The Monte Carlo method has four key stages:

1 Define a range of possible inputs
2 Generate input randomly from the domain
3 Perform deterministic computation using these inputs
4 Aggregate the results of the individual computations

TRICKS OF THE TRADE

- Stochastic modeling used to be known as “statistical sampling.” Prior to the emergence of computers, it was rarely used because of the number of calculations involved in modeling, but there are now many off-the-shelf computer applications that can handle stochastic modeling quite easily.
- The Monte Carlo model was popularized by von Neumann, Ulam, and Fermi, among others, in the 1930s. The roots of the model actually lie in physics, and the model is still widely used by scientists as well as economists.
- The Monte Carlo simulation model is often used when the model is complex, nonlinear, or involves more than just a couple of uncertain parameters. A simulation can typically involve over 10,000 evaluations of the model, a task which in the past was only practical using super computers.

MORE INFO

Book:

Morgan, Bryon J. T. *Applied Stochastic Modelling*. 2nd ed. Boca Raton, FL: Chapman & Hall/CRC, 2009.

Report:

du Toit, Barry. "Risk, theory, reflection: Limitations of the stochastic model of uncertainty in financial risk analysis." RiskWorX, June 2004. Online at: www.riskworx.com/insights/theory/theory.pdf

Stress Testing

WHAT IT MEASURES

Stress testing is a risk management tool that helps to identify how vulnerable a business, portfolio, or venture might be to unusual, negative circumstances. It may involve scenario analysis or simulation, based on hypothetical or historical data.

WHY IT IS IMPORTANT

Stress testing is extremely useful to financial analysts because it provides them with additional information on potential portfolio losses in the event of extreme, but unlikely events. Crucially, stress testing enables risk managers to test how robust a particular investment or instrument will be in the event of a serious change in circumstances.

The current "credit crunch" is a perfect example of the importance of stress testing. Institutions that conducted thorough stress tests based on a simultaneous lack of credit coupled with increased exposure to collateral debt obligations have been less seriously affected, according to financial regulators.

HOW IT WORKS IN PRACTICE

Stress testing is used to test instruments against scenarios such as: What happens if the market collapses by 60%? What happens if interest rates on our loans double? What if our lease costs increase by 75%?

The most common approach to stress testing is to use Monte Carlo simulation. This involves taking a number of randomized scenarios, ranging from modest to extreme outcomes (say a 90% drop in sales, versus a 90% increase in sales), and modeling the results on a probability distribution curve.

Most stress testing exercises involve multiple stressors. There is usually also the ability to test the current ability to cope with a known historical scenario. In recent years, many companies have tested their ability to cope with the kind of recession seen in Europe during the 1990s, for example.

There are three basic kinds of event a stress test can be applied to: Extreme event (current positions combined with historical event); risk factor shock; and external factor shock (shock of any external index factor, such as oil prices or exchange rates).

There are two basic sorts of stress test—sensitivity tests and scenario tests. A sensitivity test assesses the impact of large movement in financial variables on portfolio values without needing a specific reason. For example, you might test what happens if interest rates fall by 20%, or the cost of equity rises by 15%. Sensitivity tests can be run quickly and easily, but lack historical perspective.

Scenario tests are more costly and complex, but provide a better insight into long-term risk. They are constructed either within the context of a specific portfolio or based on a specific set of historical circumstances. Risk managers identify a portfolio's key drivers and test what happens if those drivers are stressed beyond value at risk (VAR) levels. Many risk managers use a hybrid approach of scenario and sensitivity testing.

TRICKS OF THE TRADE

- In many countries, stress testing is a regulatory requirement. In the United Kingdom, for example, the Financial Services Authority (FSA) requires certain financial institutions to conduct stress tests and ensure they have sufficient capital reserves available to handle extreme events.
- Stress testing is mostly used to analyze market risk, and the impact of market changes on portfolios such as interest rates, equity, exchange rates, and commodity instruments. These portfolios are suitable for stress testing because their market prices are regularly updated, giving sufficient data to analyze.
- VAR analysis is a very useful risk management tool, but it is not able to incorporate all possible risk outcomes, particularly sudden, dramatic changes in market circumstances.
- Stress testing is often used as a tool to communicate risk to business leaders. Rather than the hypothetical probabilities of VAR, stress testing provides a response to a very specific set of circumstances.

- Regulators commonly use stress testing to consider the vulnerability of entire financial systems. Stress tests were recently used by the Bank of England as part of a Financial Sector Assessment Program (FSAP), which considered how 10 large domestic banks would deal with a 35% decline in global stock prices, and a 12% decline in domestic property prices.

MORE INFO

Book:

Rösch, Daniel, and Harald Scheule (eds). *Stress-Testing for Financial Institutions: Applications, Regulations and Techniques*. London: Risk Books, 2009.

Article:

Bunn, Philip, Alastair Cunningham, and Mathias Drehmann. "Stress testing as a tool for assessing systemic risks." *Financial Stability Review* (June 2005). Online at: tinyurl.com/6y3e753 [PDF].

Swap Valuation

WHAT IT MEASURES

In finance, a swap is a derivative in which two parties agree to exchange one stream of cash flow against another. The swap buyer makes a stream of interest payments on a principal sum to the seller, based on the present value of the asset, for a fixed period of time. The seller then receives payments from the seller, which are usually based on a fixed rate, such as Libor. The swap valuation is the price that each party assigns to the components of the swap, and dictates the level of payments made by the buyer of the swap.

WHY IT IS IMPORTANT

Interest rate swaps were originally created to allow large corporations to avoid the cost of exchange controls. Today, they are one of the most popular and flexible financial instruments. They can be used by hedge funds to managed fixed or floating assets and liabilities, while speculators often use swaps to profit from changes in interest rates.

HOW IT WORKS IN PRACTICE

Interest rate swaps do not generate revenue themselves, they merely convert one interest rate basis to another. This type of swap is known as a "plain vanilla" swap, and is by far the most common form of swap.

Because the interest rate swap is simply a series of cash flows occurring at known future dates, it is possible to calculate its value by using a series of estimated discount cash flows.

To calculate a theoretical swap rate (TSR) for the fixed component of a swap contract, use the following formula:

$$\text{TSR} = \frac{\text{Present value of the floating rate payments}}{(\text{Notional principal}_t \times \text{days} \div 360 \times \text{df}_t)}$$

For example, company A and company B agree to a $100 million vanilla swap over three years with company A paying the swap rate, and company B paying six-month Libor floating rate.

Using the formula, it is possible to calculate a swap rate value by using the six-month Libor rate to estimate the present value of the floating rate payments.

First, calculate the present value (PV) of the payment, using Libor forward rates for three years.

As with the floating rate payments, Libor forward rates are used to discount the notional principal for the three-year period. The PV of the notional principal is calculated by multiplying the days in the period and the floating rate forward discount factor.

In our example above, the present value of the notional principal over six bi-annual payments would be calculated at $278,145,000 using the Libor forward rate to discount the cash flow.

To calculate the theoretical swap rate, we would use the following calculation:

$$\text{TSR} = \frac{12{,}816{,}663}{278{,}145{,}000} = 0.046 = 4.6\%$$

In this scenario, the buyer would therefore pay a fixed rate of 4.61% to the seller of the swap, in exchange for receiving six-month Libor interest payments.

TRICKS OF THE TRADE

- Remember, that in an interest rate swap, the principal amount is not exchanged between the counterparties. Rather, interest payments are based on a "notional amount."
- In addition, because the fixed rate component of the swap is based on the rate that values the fixed rate payments at the same present value as the variable rates, there is no advantage to either party at the time of entering a swap and no upfront payment is made. During the life of the swap, the same valuation is used, but since interest rates change, the PV of the variable rate will also change—creating an advantage for one party.
- A swap will typically last for between one and 15 years. The period of the contract is known as the swap's tenor or maturity. The counterparty paying the fixed rate is known as the buyer of the swap, while the floating-rate payer is known as the seller.

- While it is important to understand the theoretical basis of swap valuation, there are a number of computer programs that will perform complex calculations to provide highly accurate valuations.
- You may sometimes see the floating and fixed components of a swap referred to as the "legs" of the swap.

MORE INFO

Books:

Buetow, Gerald W., and Frank J. Fabozzi. *Valuation of Interest Rate Swaps and Swaptions*. New Hope, PA: Frank J. Fabozzi, 2001.

Rogers, Simon. *Swaps in Practice: The Products, Pricing and Applications*. London: Euromoney Books, 2004.

Article:

Duffie, Darrell. "Credit swap valuation." *Financial Analysts Journal* 55:1 (January/February 1999): 73–87. Preprint online at: www.defaultrisk.com/pp_crdrv_57.htm

Term Structure of Interest Rates

WHAT IT MEASURES

A mathematical description of the relationship between interest rates (or the cost of borrowing) and the time to maturity of a debt in a given currency, often used in relation to fixed securities. The resulting relationship is plotted on a graph that is known as a "yield curve." This curve can then be analyzed to measure the expected yield of securities over time.

WHY IT IS IMPORTANT

The term structure or yield curve graph shows investors how returns compare to government-issued Treasury bonds (which are considered risk-free), and how an investment compares with other fixed-income securities with the same maturity.

By observing the shape of the graph, investors can gain insight into the likely future direction of the economy and identify trading opportunities. This is important to investors but also to businesses, since most strategic business decisions depend on the availability and cost of capital—which is determined by interest rates.

HOW IT WORKS IN PRACTICE

The yield curve plots the annualized percentage increase in the yield of a specific investment. For example, if a bank account returns an interest rate of 4%, the yield is said to be 4%. However, most investments offer different returns over time. A bank may offer a higher interest rate for deposits that are invested over five years, for example.

The yield is therefore expressed as a function P(t), where t is the period of time invested over. This means that P(t) represents the value today of receiving one unit of currency t years in the future. P is usually an increasing function of t. The formula for calculating the yield (or interest term structure) for borrowing money of a period of time is as follows:

$$Y_t = \left[\frac{1}{P(t)}\right] - 1$$

The yield curve function P is actually only known with certainty for a few specific maturity dates, the other maturities are calculated by interpolation.

The simplest method of calculating the function P, and therefore the term structure of interest rates, is using the market expectations hypothesis. This states that if investors have an expectation of what one-year interest rates will be, then year-two interest rates will be calculated by compounding the first year's interest rate with the current year's. Over a longer term, rates are calculated as equal to the geometric mean of the yield on short-term rates. This information can be used to construct a simple yield curve.

TRICKS OF THE TRADE

- Critics point out this approach neglects the risk involved in bonds, while other analysts use the liquidity preference model, which includes a premium in the calculation to reflect the benefit of holding long-term bonds (the term premium). This explains the upward curve of most long-term yields.
- There are three basic patterns revealed by term structure graphs:
  a The normal yield curve: The line illustrating normal market conditions, where there are no significant changes expected to the economy and growth is fixed and predictable. In this market, fixed-income securities will likely generate higher yields the further away the maturity date.
  b The flat yield curve illustrates a market that is transitioning and where future movement is unclear, creating a flatter curve than the normal yield curve.
  c The inverted yield curve is rare and seen only during abnormal markets, where investors expect interest rates to decline over time, which will lead to lower yields further into the future.

Tick Value

WHAT IT MEASURES

There are in fact two different uses of the term "tick value."

1 Tick value can refer to the value of the minimum price movement of a traded stock allowed by an exchange. For example, many US stock markets have a tick *size* of 0.01, which translates into a tick *value* of one cent for the NYSE. In contrast, the EUR futures market has a tick value of 0.0001.
2 Tick value can also refer to the number of buyers and sellers of a stock who are bidding above or below the current market value of a stock.

WHY IT IS IMPORTANT

For traded companies, tick value is part of the contractual requirement to be listed on a stock market. Understanding tick value can also help when assessing the risk associated with investment opportunities: Markets with smaller tick values will generate smaller gains and losses with each price movement of a stock.

For investors, tick value also gives a good indication of how many investors are buying a stock on upticks versus downticks, which can be tracked over time to see whether market sentiment is broadly rising or falling.

HOW IT WORKS IN PRACTICE

Stock value relating to market sentiment is calculated according to the number of people placing orders to buy and sell a stock at any given time.

For example, at 9am Company A's stock will have a spread value, based on the difference between highest price buyers will pay, and the lowest bid sellers will accept. For frequently traded stocks, the spread will tend to be relatively small.

A buyer might believe the value of Company A's stock is increasing, and wants to buy stock now. They will therefore place an order for stock, and accept the best offer available from a seller. This sort of transaction is said to have happened on an "up tick" where the market is expected to rise. The opposite, where the seller accepts the best price offered by a buyer, is said to happen on a "down tick."

Stock exchanges calculate tick value by measuring precisely how many trades happen on each of these trajectories every few seconds. For example, on the NYSE, the tick value is taken every six seconds. A tick value of +100 means that 100 more issues traded on down ticks rather than up ticks. Tracking the tick value over time allows you to gain insight into market sentiment.

TRICKS OF THE TRADE

- Among European currency exchanges, the euro futures market has a tick value of $12.50, compared to $6.25 for the British pound futures market. Tick values in stock indexes vary widely, from $5 for the Dow Jones futures market up to $12.50 for the S&P 500.
- Some statisticians have attempted to use tick data to analyze market performance and make predictions based on average ticks over 20 days. Generally speaking, ticks of more than +1000 or less than −800 would suggest excessive market optimism or pessimism.

MORE INFO

Articles:

Porter, David C., and Daniel G. Weaver. "Tick size and market quality." *Financial Management* 26:4 (Winter 1997): 5–26.

Small Investors Software Co. "NYSE tick—Statistical analysis." July 3, 2003. Online at: tinyurl.com/6g8ar8s (via Internet Archive).

Steenbarger, Brett. "A NYSE TICK primer: How to assess intraday sentiment." *TraderFeed* (December 16, 2008). Online at: tinyurl.com/5wcfp6

Time Value of Money

WHAT IT MEASURES

Time Value of Money (TVM) is one of the most important concepts in the financial world. If a business is paid $1 million for something today, that money is worth more than if the same $1 million was paid at some point in the future. The reason money given today is worth more is straightforward: If I have money today, I have the potential to earn interest on the capital.

TVM values how much more a given sum of money is worth now (or at a specific future date) compared to in the future (or, in the case of a future payment, a date that is even further in the future). TVM calculations take into account likely interest gains, discounted cash flow, and potential risk, to create a value figure for a specific amount of money or investment opportunity.

There are several calculations commonly used to express the time value of money, but the most important are present value and future value.

WHY IT IS IMPORTANT

If company A has the opportunity to realize $10,000 from an asset today, or two years in the future, TVM allows the company to calculate exactly how much more that $10,000 is worth if it's received today, as opposed to in the future. It is important to know how to calculate the time value of money because it means you can distinguish between the value of investment opportunities that offer returns at different times.

HOW IT WORKS IN PRACTICE

If a business has the option of receiving a $1 million investment today or a guaranteed payment of the same amount in two years' time, you can use TVM calculations to show the relative value of the two sums of money.

Option A, take the money now: The business might accept the $1,000,000 investment immediately and put the capital into an account paying a 4.5% annual return. In this account, the

$1,000,000 would earn $92,025 interest over two years (annually compounded), making the future value of the investment $1,092,025. This can be expressed using the following formula:

$$\text{Future value} = 1{,}000{,}000 \times (1 + 0.045)^2$$

which might be expressed as:

$$\text{Future value} = \text{Original sum} \times (1 + \text{Interest rate per period})^{\text{No of periods}}$$

Obviously, the present value of the $1 million if it is received today would be $1 million. But if the money isn't received for another two years, we can still calculate its present and future values.

The present value of a future $1 million investment is based on how much you would need to receive today to receive $1 million in two years' time. This is done by discounting the $1,000,000 by the interest rate for the period. Assuming an annual interest rate of 4.5%, we can calculate the present value using the following formula:

$$\text{Present value} = \frac{\text{Future value}}{(1 + \text{Interest rate per period})^{\text{No of periods}}}$$

Using this formula, we can see that the present value of a future payment of $1 million in two years' time is:

$$\frac{1{,}000{,}000}{(1 + 0.045)^2} = \$915{,}730$$

In other words, the investment in two years time is the equivalent of receiving $915,730 today, and investing it at 4.5% for two years.

TRICKS OF THE TRADE

- There are five key components in TVM calculations. These are: present value, future value, the number of periods, the interest rate, and a payment principal sum. Providing you know four of these values, you can rearrange the TVM formulae to calculate the fifth.

- When calculating TVM, you may sometimes need to supplement the calculation to discount future payments to take account of risk as well as time value. Discount rates can be adjusted to take account of risks like the other party not paying you back (default risk) or the fact that the item you intended to purchase has become more expensive, reducing the buying power of the money. In this case, the company lending the principal sum might insist on a higher interest rate to compensate for the risk.
- If a future payment is not certain, you can use the capital asset pricing model to calculate the risk involved.

MORE INFO

Websites:

Money-zine TVM calculator: tinyurl.com/6cmtjql

TVMCalcs.com guide: www.tvmcalcs.com/tvm/tvm_intro

See Also:

Future Value (pp. 149–150)

Total Return

Total return is one more way to evaluate investment decisions, and because it totals all factors it is perhaps a calculation that investors value most—or should.

WHAT IT MEASURES

The total percentage change in the value of an investment over a specified time period, including capital gains, dividends, and the investment's appreciation or depreciation.

WHY IT IS IMPORTANT

Total return furnishes fundamental information that every investor seeks sooner or later: All things considered, just how much did my investment return?

That in itself makes total return rather important. In addition, there are several sound reasons for paying close attention to each of its components. For those who invest to maximize income, dividends will be very important. For those who invest for long-term growth, capital appreciation will be equally important.

Knowing how much of an investment's total return is attributable to each of the components can help in assessing how volatile the fund is likely to be, how tax-efficient it is, and how much steady income it can be expected to produce.

HOW IT WORKS IN PRACTICE

The total return formula reflects all the ways in which an investment may earn or lose money: dividends as income, capital gains distributions, and capital appreciation—the increase or decrease in the investment's net asset value (NAV):

$$\text{Total return} = \frac{(\text{Dividends} + \text{Capital gains distributions} \pm \text{Change in NAV})}{\text{Initial NAV}}$$

If, for instance, you buy a stock with an initial NAV of $40, and after one year it pays an income dividend of $2 per share and a capital gains distribution of $1, and its NAV has increased to $42, then the stock's total return would be:

$$\frac{(2+1+2)}{40}=\frac{5}{40}=0.125=12.5\%$$

TRICKS OF THE TRADE

- The total return time-frame is usually one year, and it assumes that dividends have been reinvested.
- If a fund's capital gains exceed its capital losses for the year, most of the net gain must be distributed to stockholders as a capital gains distribution.
- Total return measures past performance only; it cannot predict future results.
- Total return generally does not take into account any sales charges that an investor paid to invest in a fund, or taxes he or she might owe on the income dividends and capital gains distributions received.
- Rules of the US Securities & Exchange Commission require a company to show a comparison of the total return on its common stock for the last five fiscal years with the total returns of a broad market index and a more narrowly focused industry or group index.
- Total return can be a key yardstick in selecting funds once an investor has set objectives and a time horizon, and made decisions about risk and reward.

Treynor Ratio

WHAT IT MEASURES

The Treynor ratio, as devised by Jack Treynor, is a measurement of a portfolio's return earned in excess of what would be earned on a risk-free investment. The higher the Treynor ratio, the better the performance of the portfolio or stock being analyzed.

WHY IT IS IMPORTANT

The Treynor ratio is used to calculate returns over and above what would be generated by a risk-free investment. Whenever the Treynor ratio is high, it denotes that the investor received high yields for each unit of market risk. One of the key advantages of Treynor is that it shows how a fund will perform not in relation to its own volatility but the volatility it brings to an overall portfolio.

HOW IT WORKS IN PRACTICE

The Treynor Ratio divides a portfolio's excess return by its "beta." This is the widely used measure of market-related risk in a stock or collection of stocks. If a stock has a beta of 0.5, it tends to move up or down with the market, but only half as far as the overall market. If a stock has a beta of 1.25 and the market moves up by 10%, that stock would move up by 12.5%.

The formula for the Treynor Ratio is as follows:

$$\text{Treynor ratio} = \frac{\text{(Average portfolio return} - \text{Average risk return of risk-free investment)}}{\text{Beta of portfolio}}$$

The formula can be applied to any fund or portfolio where you can find a beta value—the beta is a measurement of market-related risk.

An investor might use the Treynor ratio to calculate the return generated by a fund over the return of short-term Treasury bills. If the fund returns 12% over three years, while the Treasury bill rate is 1.5% and the fund's beta is 0.5, then we can see the Treynor ratio is: (12 – 1.5) ÷ 0.5 = 21.

TRICKS OF THE TRADE

- Like the Sharpe ratio, the Treynor ratio doesn't quantify the value added—it is simply a ranking mechanism. Where the two mechanisms differ is that the Sharpe ratio considers total risk (the standard deviation of the portfolio) while the Treynor ratio considers systematic risk (the beta of a portfolio versus the benchmark).
- In practice, it's possible to simply look up Treynor ratios for many listed equity funds. For example, many newspapers and financial websites will list Treynor figures under "performance" data, usually over three, five, and 10 years.
- It is worth considering how Treynor Ratios change over time and in relation to similar funds—a three-year ratio may be negative while five-year and 10-year figures are positive. This could be because the fund is mismanaged but also could reflect a market downturn or a short-term problem.

MORE INFO

See Also:

Risk-Adjusted Rate of Return (pp. 231–233)
Sharpe Ratio (pp. 237–238)

Value at Risk

WHAT IT MEASURES

Value at risk (VAR) is a useful tool for anyone looking to quantify the risk of a particular project or investment opportunity by measuring the potential loss that might be incurred over a certain period of time. VAR measures what is the most that an investor might lose, based on a specific level of confidence, over a specific period of time. For example, "What's the most I can—with a 95% level of confidence—expect to lose over the next 12 months?"

WHY IT IS IMPORTANT

Most risk measurements focus on volatility whereas VAR focuses specifically on losses. It is commonly used to evaluate risk across a portfolio, but can also be applied to single indexes or anything that trades like a stock. VAR is important because it provides financial executives with a method of quantifying risk that is rigorous but also easily understood by nonfinancial executives.

HOW IT WORKS IN PRACTICE

The most common method of calculating VAR is the variance-covariance approach, sometimes referred to as "parametric VAR." Parametric VAR is a percentile-based risk measure that measures the expected loss of a portfolio over a specific period of time, depending on the confidence. To calculate parametric VAR, use the following formula:

$$\text{Value at risk} = \text{Mean} \times \text{HPR} + [\text{Z} - \text{score} \times \text{Std Dev} \times \text{SQRT (HPR)}]$$

where Mean is the average expected (or actual) rate of return, HPR is the holding period, Z-score is the probability, Std Dev is the standard deviation, and SQRT is the square root (of time).

To calculate the VAR of a portfolio worth $1 million with an expected average annual return of 13%, a standard annual deviation of 20% (equal to a daily deviation of 1.26%), and a 95% confidence score, therefore, you would perform the following calculation:

13 × 1 + (95 × 1.26 × SQRT) = 6.037%

This results in a 10-day VAR of $60,370. This means that your biggest potential loss over any 10-day period should not exceed $60,370 more than 5% of the time, or approximately once a year.

TRICKS OF THE TRADE

- VAR is now increasingly accepted as the *de facto* standard for risk measurement. In 1993, when the Bank of International Settlements members met in Basel, they amended the Basel Accord to require banks to hold in reserve enough capital to cover 10 days of losses based on a 95% 10-day VAR.
- A simpler alternative approach to calculating VAR is using the historical method—this simply takes all empirical profit and loss history and puts the returns in order of size. If we had 100 historical returns, the VAR for a 99% confidence score would simply be the second largest loss. Critics argue that very few portfolios have enough historical data to make this approach reliable, however.
- A third approach to calculating VAR is the simulation or Monte Carlo method, which uses computerized simulation to generate thousands of possible returns from a parametric assumption, then ordering them in the same way as with an historical calculation.
- Although VAR is often described as the "maximum possible" loss, this only applies at a single percentage confidence score. It is always possible to lose more by applying a higher confidence level—this is known as the conditional value at risk (CVAR), expected shortfall, or extreme tail loss.

MORE INFO

Books:

Butler, Cormac. *Mastering Value at Risk: A Step-by-Step Guide to Understanding and Applying VAR*. London: FT Prentice Hall, 1999.

Choudhry, Moorad. *An Introduction to Value-at-Risk*. 5th ed. Chichester, UK: Wiley, 2013.

Article:

Harper, David. "An introduction to value at risk (VAR)." *Investopedia* (May 27, 2010). Online at: www.investopedia.com/articles/04/092904.asp

Website:

Risk Glossary on VAR: www.riskglossary.com/link/value_at_risk.htm

See Also:

Earnings at Risk (pp. 119–120)

Weighted Average Cost of Capital

WHAT IT MEASURES

The weighted average cost of capital (WACC) is the rate of return that the providers of a company's capital require, weighted according to the proportion each element bears to the total pool of capital.

WHY IT IS IMPORTANT

WACC is one of the most important figures in assessing a company's financial health, both for internal use (in capital budgeting) and external use (valuing companies on investment markets). It gives companies an insight into the cost of their financing, can be used as a hurdle rate for investment decisions, and acts as a measure to be minimized to find the best possible capital structure for the company. WACC is a rough guide to the rate of interest per monetary unit of capital. As such, it can be used to provide a discount rate for cash flows with similar risk to that of the overall business.

HOW IT WORKS IN PRACTICE

To calculate the weighted average cost of capital, companies must multiply the cost of each element of capital for a project—which may include loans, bonds, equity, and preferred stock—by its percentage of the total capital, and then add them together.

For example, a business might consider investing $40 million in an expansion program. The financing is raised through a combination of equity (such as $10m of stock with an expected 10% return) and debt (for example, $30m bond issue, with 5% coupon).

In this simple scenario, WACC would be calculated as follows:

Equity ($10m) divided by total capital ($40m)
= 25%, multiplied by cost of equity (10%) = 2.5%
Debt ($30m) divided by total capital ($40m)
= 75%, multiplied by cost of debt (5%) = 3.75%

The two results added together give a weighted cost of capital of 6.25%.

In reality, interest payments are tax deductible, so a more accurate formula for WACC is:

$$WACC = DP \times DC - T + EP \times EC$$

where DP is the proportion of debt financing, DC is the cost of debt financing, T is the company's tax rate, EP is the proportion of equity finance, and EC is the cost of equity finance.

TRICKS OF THE TRADE

- To accurately calculate WACC, you need to know the specific rates of return required for each source of capital. For example, different sources of finance may attract different levels of taxation, or interest, which should be accounted for. A true WACC calculation could therefore be much more complex than the example provided here.
- Critics of WACC argue that financial analysts rely on it too heavily, and that the algorithm should not be used to assess risky projects, where the cost of capital will necessarily be higher to reflect the higher risk.
- Investors use WACC to help decide whether a company represents a good investment opportunity. To some extent, WACC represents the rate at which a company produces value for investors—if a company produces a return of 20% and has a WACC of 11%, then the company creates 9% additional value for investors. If the return is lower than the WACC, the business is unlikely to secure investment.

- Although the WACC formula seems simple, different analysts will often come up with different WACC calculations for the same company depending on how they interpret the company's debt, market value, and interest rates.

MORE INFO

Book:

Pratt, Shannon P., and Roger J. Grabowski. *Cost of Capital: Applications and Examples*. Hoboken, NJ: Wiley, 2008.

Websites:

Money Terms on WACC: moneyterms.co.uk/wacc/
12 Manage on WACC: www.12manage.com/methods_wacc.html

Working Capital

Working capital is concrete proof of the business axiom "It takes money to make money."

WHAT IT MEASURES

The funds that are readily available to operate a business. Working capital comprises the total net current assets of a business, which are its inventory, debtors, and cash—minus its creditors.

WHY IT IS IMPORTANT

Obviously, it is vital for a company to have sufficient working capital to meet all of its requirements. The faster a business expands, the greater will be its working capital needs.

If current assets do not exceed current liabilities, a company may well run into trouble paying creditors who want their money quickly. Indeed, the leading cause of business failure is not lack of profitability, but rather lack of working capital, which helps to explain why some experts advise: "Use someone else's money every chance you get, and don't let anyone else use yours."

HOW IT WORKS IN PRACTICE

Working capital is also called net current assets or current capital, and is expressed as:

Working capital = Current assets − Current liabilities

Current assets are cash and assets that can be converted to cash within one year or a normal operating cycle; current liabilities are monies owed that are due within one year.

If a company's current assets total $300,000 and its current liabilities total $160,000, its working capital is:

300,000 − 160,000 = $140,000

The working capital cycle describes capital (usually cash) as it moves through a company: It first flows from a company to pay for supplies, materials, finished goods inventory, and wages to workers who produce goods and services. It then flows into a company as goods and services are sold and as new investment equity and loans are received. Each stage of this cycle consumes time. The more time the stages consume, the greater the demands on working capital.

TRICKS OF THE TRADE

- Good management of working capital includes actions like collecting receivables faster and moving inventory more quickly; generating more cash increases working capital.
- While it can be tempting to use cash to pay for fixed assets like computers or vehicles, doing so reduces the amount of cash available for working capital.
- If working capital is tight, consider other ways of financing capital investment, such as loans, fresh equity, or leasing.
- Early warning signs of insufficient working capital include pressure on existing cash; exceptional cash-generating activities such as offering high discounts for early payment; increasing lines of credit; partial payments to suppliers and creditors; a preoccupation with surviving rather than managing; frequent short-term emergency requests to the bank, for example, to help pay wages, pending receipt of a check.
- Several ratios measure how effectively and efficiently working capital is being used. These ratios are explained separately.

MORE INFO

Websites:

PlanWare on working capital: www.planware.org/workingcapital.htm

Study Finance on working capital management: www.studyfinance.com/lessons/workcap/

See Also:

Working Capital Cycle (pp. 270–272)
Working Capital Productivity (pp. 273–274)

Working Capital Cycle

WHAT IT MEASURES

The working capital cycle measures the amount of time that elapses between the moment when your business begins investing money in a product or service, and the moment the business receives payment for that product or service. This doesn't necessarily begin when you manufacture a product—businesses often invest money in products when they hire people to produce goods, or when they buy raw materials.

WHY IT IS IMPORTANT

A good working capital cycle balances incoming and outgoing payments to maximize working capital. Simply put, you need to know you can afford to research, produce, and sell your product.

A short working capital cycle suggests a business has good cash flow. For example, a company that pays contractors in 7 days but takes 30 days to collect payments has 23 days of working capital to fund—also known as having a working capital cycle of 23 days. Amazon.com, in contrast, collects money before it pays for goods. This means the company has a negative working capital cycle and has more capital available to fund growth. For a business to grow, it needs access to cash—and being able to free up cash from the working capital cycle is cheaper than other sources of finance, such as loans.

HOW IT WORKS IN PRACTICE

The key to understanding a company's working capital cycle is to know where payments are collected and made, and to identify areas where the cycle is stretched—and can potentially be reduced.

The working capital cycle is a diagram rather than a mathematical calculation. The cycle shows all the cash coming in to the business, what it is used for, and how it leaves the business (i.e., what it is spent on).

A simple working capital cycle diagram is shown in Figure 1. The arrows in the diagram show the movement of assets through the business—including cash, but also other assets such as raw materials and finished goods. Each item represents a reservoir of assets—for example, cash into the business is converted into labor. The working capital cycle will break down if there is not a supply of assets moving continually through the cycle (known as a liquidity crisis).

Figure 1. A simple working capital cycle diagramWorking capital cycle

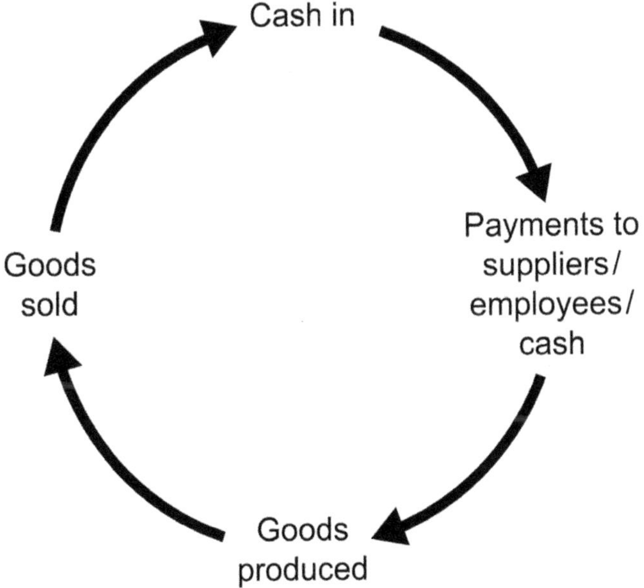

The working capital diagram should be customized to show the way capital moves around your business. More complex diagrams might include incoming assets such as cash payments, interest payments, loans, and equity. Items that commonly absorb cash would be labor, inventory, and suppliers.

The key thing to model is the time lag between each item on the diagram. For some businesses, there may be a very long delay between making the product and receiving cash from sales. Others may need to purchase raw materials a long time before the product can be manufactured. Once you have this information, it is possible to calculate your total working capital cycle, and potentially identify where time lags within the cycle can be reduced or eliminated.

TRICKS OF THE TRADE

- For investors, the working capital cycle is most relevant when analyzing capital-intensive businesses where cash flow is used to buy inventory. Typically, the working capital cycle of retailers, consumer goods, and consumer goods manufacturers is critical to their success.
- The working capital cycle should be considered alongside the cash conversion cycle—a measure of working capital efficiency that gives clues about the average number of days that working capital is invested in the operating cycle.

MORE INFO

Article:

Harper, David. "Financial statements: Working capital." *Investopedia*. Online at: tinyurl.com/5sgvfau

See Also:

Working Capital (pp. 268–269)
Working Capital Productivity (pp. 273–274)

Working Capital Productivity

However expressed or calculated, working capital productivity is a measurement that offers a snapshot of a company's efficiency by comparing working capital with sales or turnover.

WHAT IT MEASURES

How effectively a company's management is using its working capital.

WHY IT IS IMPORTANT

It is obvious that capital not being put to work properly is being wasted, which is certainly not in investors' best interests.

As an expression of how effectively a company spends its available funds compared with sales or turnover, the working capital productivity figure helps to establish a clear relationship between its financial performance and process improvement. The relationship is said to have been first observed by the US management consultant George Stalk while working in Japan.

A seldom-used reciprocal calculation, the working capital turnover or working capital to sales ratio, expresses the same relationship in a different way.

HOW IT WORKS IN PRACTICE

To calculate working capital productivity, first subtract current liabilities from current assets, which is the formula for working capital, then divide this figure into sales for the period.

$$\text{Working capital productivity} = \frac{\text{Sales}}{(\text{Current assets} - \text{Current liabilities})}$$

If sales are $3,250, current assets are $900, and current liabilities are $650, then:

$$\frac{3250}{(900 - 650)} = \frac{3250}{250} = 13$$

In this case, the higher the number the better. Sales growing faster than the resources required to generate them is a clear sign of efficiency and, by definition, productivity.

The working capital to sales ratio uses the same figures, but in reverse:

$$\text{Working capital/sales ratio} = \frac{\text{Working capital}}{\text{Sales}}$$

Using the same figures in the example above, this ratio would be calculated:

$$\frac{250}{3250} = 0.077 = 7.7\%$$

For this ratio, obviously, the lower the number the better.

TRICKS OF THE TRADE

- By itself, a single ratio means little; a series of them—several quarters' worth, for example—indicates a trend, and means a great deal.
- Some experts recommend doing quarterly calculations and averaging them for a given year to arrive at the most reliable number.
- Either ratio also helps a management compare its performance with that of competitors.
- These ratios should also help to motivate companies to improve processes, such as eliminating steps in the handling of materials and bill collection, and shortening product design times. Such improvements reduce costs and make working capital available for other tasks.

MORE INFO

See Also:

Working Capital (pp. 268–269)
Working Capital Cycle (pp. 270–272)

Yield

WHAT IT MEASURES

Stocks that pay dividends (note that not all do) will produce an annual cash return to the investor. Simply dividing this cash return by the current stock price and expressing that as a percentage is known as the "yield"—that is, the annual percentage income at the current price. As far as newspapers are concerned, the yield figure they publish is usually the historical one.

Analysts will often provide forecasts for dividends in terms of earnings per share (EPS), and thus the forecast yield can then be calculated. Forecasts can, of course, go wrong, and consequently there is some risk in relying on them.

WHY IT IS IMPORTANT

Yield, after the price/earnings ratio, is one of the most common methods of comparing the relative value of stocks, and that is why it is so widely quoted in the press. The majority of investors like to see a cash income from their stocks, although to some extent this is a cultural thing. There are more companies in the United States, for example, that pay no dividends than in the United Kingdom.

HOW IT WORKS IN PRACTICE

You can compare yields against the market average or against a sector average, which in turn gives you some idea of the relative value of the stock against its peers, much like other ratios. Other things being equal, a higher-yield stock is preferable to that of an identical company with a lower yield. The higher-yield stock is cheaper. In practice, of course, there may well be good reasons why the market has decided that the higher yielder should be so—possibly it has worse prospects, is less profitable, and so on. This is not always the case; the market is far from being a perfectly rational place.

An additional feature of the yield (unlike many of the other stock analysis ratios) is that it enables comparison with cash. When you put cash into an interest-bearing source like a bank account or a government stock, you get a yield—the annual interest payable. This is usually a pretty safe investment. You can compare the yield from this cash investment with the yield on stocks, which are far riskier. This produces a valuable basis for stock evaluation. If, for example, you can get 4% in a bank without capital risk, you can then look at stocks and ask yourself how this yield compares—given that, as well as the opportunity for long-term growth of both the stock price and the dividends, there is plenty of capital risk.

TRICKS OF THE TRADE

- Care is necessary, however, because unlike banks paying interest, companies are under no obligation to pay dividends at all. Frequently, if they go through a bad patch, even the largest and best-known household name companies will cut dividends or even abandon paying them altogether. So, stock yield is much less reliable than bank interest or government stock interest yield.
- Despite this, yield is an immensely useful feature of stock appraisal. It is the only ratio that tells you about the cash return to the investor, and you cannot argue with cash. EPS, for example, is subject to accountants' opinions, but a dividend once paid is an unarguable fact.

MORE INFO

See Also:

Bond Yield (pp. 38–40)
Dividend Yield (pp. 116–118)

Z-Score

WHAT IT MEASURES

The z-score is a measure of the financial health of a company. Devised in the 1960s by Edward Altman, the score uses statistical techniques to predict the likelihood that a company will fail because of bankruptcy within two years.

The z-score was originally created based on Altman's analysis of 33 bankrupt manufacturing companies with assets averaging $6.4 million and a further 33 nonbankrupt companies with assets between $1 million and $25 million. Altman's analysis showed that 95% of the bankrupt companies had a z-score that suggested financial problems.

WHY IT IS IMPORTANT

Since the 1980s, auditors have used the z-score to help identify companies with serious cash problems. The measure is also used to help score applicants for loans. Stockbrokers commonly use the z-score to determine if a company is a good investment.

HOW IT WORKS IN PRACTICE

The z-score combines five common business ratios and uses a weighting system devised by Altman to produce a score somewhere between −4 and +8. Each of the components that make up the final z-score are rated independently, and each component has a different weight in the calculation of the overall z-score. The exact emphasis on each factor can vary slightly from one industry to another, using more specific z-score calculators.

All the information needed to calculate a z-score is available in company financial reports. The original formula to calculate a z-score is as follows:

$$z = 1.2T1 + 1.4T2 + 3.3T3 + 0.6T4 + 0.999T5$$

where:
T1 = working capital ÷ total assets

T2 = retained earnings ÷ total assets
T3 = earnings before interest and tax ÷ total assets
T4 = market value of equity ÷ book value of total liabilities
T5 = sales ÷ total assets
A score can be analyzed as follows:
$>$ 2.99: the company is considered "safe"
1.8–2.99: there is some risk of financial distress
$<$ 1.8: there is serious risk of financial distress

TRICKS OF THE TRADE

- Although the numbers that go into the z-score can be influenced by external events, it is a useful tool to provide a quick analysis of where a company stands compared to competitors, and for tracking the risk of insolvency over time.
- Studies have shown the z-score is an accurate prediction of company failure rates in between seven and eight out of 10 cases.
- The formula was originally devised to be used for public companies, but amendments have since been made to allow z-scores to be calculated for privately held companies. In this case, the calculation that should be used is as follows: $0.717T1 + 0.87T2 + 0.420T4 + 0.998T5$

For private companies, a score of 2.9 is "safe," while a score below 1.23 is considered a serious risk of financial distress.

MORE INFO

Book:

Altman, Edward I. "The z-score bankruptcy model: Past, present, and future." In Edward I. Altman and Arnold W. Sametz (eds). *Financial Crises: Institutions and Markets in a Fragile Environment*. New York: Wiley, 1977.

Website:

EasyCalculation.com z-score business health calculator: easycalculation.com/statistics/altman-z-score.php

www.ingramcontent.com/pod-product-compliance
Ingram Content Group UK Ltd.
Pitfield, Milton Keynes, MK11 3LW, UK
UKHW020224250726
13967UKWH00001B/181

9 781849 300681